I Left My Toxic Relationship – Now What?

I LEFT MY TOXIC RELATIONSHIP

Now What?

THE STEP-BY-STEP GUIDE
TO STARTING OVER
AND LIVING ON YOUR OWN

HEATHER J. KENT

NEW YORK

LONDON • NASHVILLE • MELBOURNE • VANCOUVER

I LEFT MY TOXIC RELATIONSHIP – *Now What?*

The Step-By-Step Guide to Starting Over and Living on Your Own

Published in New York, New York, by Morgan James Publishing in partnership with Difference Press. Morgan James is a trademark of Morgan James, LLC. www.MorganJamesPublishing.com

ISBN 9781642799873 paperback
ISBN 9781642799880 eBook
ISBN 9781642799897 audio
Library of Congress Control Number: 2020933247

Cover Design: Christopher Kirk www.GFSstudio.com

Interior Design: Chris Treccani www.3dogcreative.net

Editor: Moriah Howell

Book Coaching: The Author Incubator

Morgan James is a proud partner of Habitat for Humanity Peninsula and Greater Williamsburg. Partners in building since 2006.

Get involved today! Visit
MorganJamesPublishing.com/giving-back

*For Ellen, the most courageous warrior
I have ever known. Namaste.*

Table of Contents

Chapter 1:   Floating on a Raft   1

Chapter 2:   My Story of Surviving and Starting Over   7

Chapter 3:   So ... Now What?   21

Chapter 4:   Roadblocks   27

Chapter 5:   Taking Care of Yourself
                (And Why It Matters)   35

Chapter 6:   The Lies We Believe   53

Chapter 7:   Overcoming Fear   67

Chapter 8:   Driving the Emotional Roller Coaster   81

Chapter 9:   Making Connections   97

Chapter 10:   "Who Am I, Anyway?"   107

Chapter 11:   Finding Your Voice   117

Chapter 12:   The Bumps and the Potholes   127

Chapter 13:   From Pain to Power and Purpose   137

Acknowledgments   143

Thank You   147

About the Author   149

Chapter 1:

FLOATING ON A RAFT

Do you remember that scene from *Castaway* when Chuck Noland (played by Tom Hanks) is floating on a raft he built in the middle of the ocean? If you've never seen this movie, this is your spoiler alert. After surviving a brutal plane crash and washing up on a deserted island, Chuck spends the next several years learning how to adapt and survive in his new and, at times, hostile and unforgiving environment. (He also creates a character out of a *Wilson*-brand soccer ball that washed up with him, and Wilson becomes his trusted confidant and the externalization of that nagging voice in his head). He tries multiple times to find a way to leave the island, but the surf is too strong to overcome. As the years go by, he realizes that no one will ever find him there, so he engineers a really sweet raft with a sail. He straps down all the provisions that he can, attaches Wilson to the raft, and paddles out to the breakwaters. He finally overcomes the powerful waves with the help of his sail and leaves that deserted island he was stranded on for so many years. Then, he's floating out in the middle of the ocean, alone on a raft. As the days go by at sea, I can't help but wonder if he thought, at some point, "How did I get here?"

That feeling of being alone on a life raft, suddenly in the middle of a vast ocean and wondering how you got there, feels very similar to how it feels immediately after leaving an abusive, toxic relationship. It's scary and unknown, incredibly vast (like the ocean), and sometimes insurmountable. Even though the environment we were living in before was hostile, damaging, and unforgiving (like that deserted island), it was something that became familiar. We knew, more or less, how to adapt our behaviour to survive the situation. But then, something deep inside of us kept telling us that there is more to life than staying on that deserted island of abuse and emotional turmoil. We decided to finally make a break for it, and now that we are floating on this life raft with infinity facing us in all directions, things are feeling *really* freaking uncomfortable and really, really scary. We might start to have thoughts like, "What am I doing? Why did I ever think this was a good idea? Who do I think I am? I can't do this on my own (*oh*, my gosh… I'm a co-dependent mess), I will never survive this," and, especially, "What do I do *now*?"

Time to Think

When you're on a raft in the middle of the ocean, there is nothing but time to think and ruminate over what happened. Questions like, "Was it all my fault? What will my family and friends think?" may start to set in, causing all kinds of worry, anxiety, and panic. My quick answers to these questions, respectively, are *no*, it was not all your fault-not at all-and it really doesn't matter what your family thinks, because they did not have to live in your shoes. Of course, it would be much easier to have an understanding and supportive family, but *not* having that isn't a good reason to stay stranded on that island. Maybe your kids are on that raft with you, and you're worried about the impact that all this will have on them. Let me calm your fears around this. First, leaving a toxic relationship where you, as their mother, are being disrespected and poorly treated is setting a wonderful example for them to learn that *they* do not have to stay in a bad relationship when someone is treating them poorly. You are showing them that standing up for yourself and protecting your loved ones is important. Second, I promise you that children will thrive much better when they have a parent who is feeling safe, secure, and grounded rather than living in fear and constant turmoil. Leaving a toxic and abusive relationship is *not* going to ruin their lives. Rather, it's going to increase their chances of developing healthy relationships with other people by teaching them that boundaries and basic respect are important.

Perhaps the biggest questions that come to mind while floating on that life raft are, "Who am I, and what do I want for my life? How do even go about living on my own?" Your mind gets flooded with thoughts about money, housing, custody, and kids' well-being (if you have kids). Maybe you think about learning how to cook, how to operate power tools or a lawnmower, and (my personal favourite) "I'm going to die alone" ... all the things. Then you start wishing that you had it all figured out and that you were already independent and living on your own ... happy, healthy, and thriving in your new life. It all feels *really* overwhelming and impossible on that life raft. I know this because I've been there too.

You're Not Alone

I have good news for you, though. You're not alone on that life raft. There are millions of women who were also on that life raft, floating away from their old life where they were stuck in a toxic relationship, and towards a new life that is unchartered and unknown. Yes, it feels completely terrifying at first. Yes, there are parts of reclaiming independence and starting over on your own that are *really* stressful and hard. Yes, there are days when you feel like giving up and just crying in a ball on the bathroom floor for hours. But, there are also days when you feel more alive than you have in as long as you can remember. There are moments when you figure out how to do something new, all by yourself (like learning how to use a cordless drill, for example), that makes you feel like you've won an Olympic Gold medal. There are skills and strategies that you will learn that will help you to navigate all those intrusive feelings and thoughts that are still flooding into your mind. There are tools (both literally and figuratively) that you can draw from to help you to heal your war wounds and build your new life.

You built that life raft for a reason; you broke free from the shackles of that deserted island and decided to get away-and you *made* it. You've already done the hardest part. Now you need to figure out what to do next-how to start your life over and live independently again, on your own. Once you've got that sorted, your life can truly become anything you want it to be. That sounds cheesy, I know. But I also know, from experience, that it's true. I am on that life raft with you now, and I will not abandon you. I am here to help you navigate these unchartered waters, find solid ground again, and share with you the skills that you need to start living and thriving in your new life of freedom and independence. I am here for *you*, girlfriend, and I promise you that you've got this!

Chapter 2:

MY STORY OF SURVIVING AND STARTING OVER

If this is your first time meeting me, you might be wondering, "Who is this girl, and what does she know about anything that I'm going through?" Valid question, so allow me to introduce myself and share my story with you. If you're reading this book, you already know my name (nice to meet you). I grew up in the Canadian province of Nova Scotia (quick geography lesson-Nova Scotia is located in the North Atlantic Ocean. It is a peninsula north of the state of Maine). I was very fortunate to have a pretty "normal" childhood (if you call your dad being an Anglican priest and your mom being a school vice-principal normal), and my parents did everything they could to support my older sister and me in our academics and our interests outside of school. When I graduated from high school, I moved four provinces away to go to university. I moved all the way to Kingston, Ontario, where I studied French, history, and education concurrently at Queen's University.

It was at the end of my first year at Queen's when I got together with a guy from my hometown, who I knew since I was in grade seven. He was also in Kingston at the same time, attending a different post-secondary school. Oddly, there were a lot of people from my little Cape Breton high school who ended up in Kingston (2,500 kilometers away from home), attending one of the several educational institutions there, so we all began to hang out about once a week a few months into my freshman year. I knew that this guy (we'll call him Mike) was interested in me as more than friends-he began to call me and leave messages, but I didn't return them. I wasn't interested at first because Mike had a bad reputation for being a player (and a jerk to girls), and he hurt a couple of friends of mine over the years. It was a red flag that I did not ignore at first. But, as the year went on, I also saw a kind, fun, and sweet side of him. So, at the end of the year, just before my final exams, I agreed to go on a date. That was that.

As you can imagine, there were lots of red flags, even in the first year of our relationship. He would tell me that he would call at a certain time, and I would be waiting by the phone. He never had a reason for not calling when he said he would- he just didn't. He even kept me waiting for the whole day of my sister's wedding rehearsal and dinner, which he told me he would attend. When he finally called in the late afternoon, he reported that he was feeling bored. He had been at home for hours and didn't bother to call. It was clear to my family that he had no respect for me or my time. For some reason, though, I didn't end it there when I normally would have. I accepted his behaviour and allowed him to continue doing things like this for years. He learned that I would tolerate it and stick around.

He also had a number of "on-call" girls on standby at any given time. He talked to them constantly online and hooked up with one of them at bar when *we* were out together with friends. I would call him out on this behaviour, but every time I did, he denied his behaviour and got so angry and I ended up feeling like I did something wrong, and I would apologize to *him*. Very early on, he learned that I was afraid when he got angry. Getting angry was a way that he could control me and the situation and turn it around to make it seem like the argument was my fault. I continued to let it happen. When I had his attention, things were great and I loved who he was; this feeling is what I so desperately clung onto when things were bad. What I was too naïve to realize at that time was that he would never change and that I was clinging to something that was only a fragment of what I deserved.

As the years went on, the problems increased to the point where I became so suspicious of him that I felt like I was going "crazy." By this point, we were living together with other roommates. He would leave his computer on, presumably so that I would see all the old girlfriends and previous casual hookups he was talking to so that it would hurt me, and I took the bait. This was how I discovered that he planned to meet up with one of them (presumably not just to have coffee) while I was at one of my part-time jobs. He would ask me to do things that these other girls used to do with him, and it made me feel incredibly degraded. I felt like I was being compared to these other girls, and I was not measuring up in the physical intimacy department. He began staying up late to watch pornography on his computer while I was in bed alone. By this point, my self-esteem plummeted to non-existent. The porn thing soon became a habit. I told him I was concerned that he had an addiction; he laughed at me and told me I was just a prude and that looking at porn was normal. While that is true, I also knew that watching it for hours every single night *by yourself* when you live with your girlfriend is not.

He made time for his friends, playing late night hockey, coaching a hockey team, and watching hours of porn. When I complained about not getting to spend much time with him, he again made it seem like my feelings were the problem and it was my fault. We were engaged by this point, and, finally, when he didn't come home at all one night, I told him that I could not marry him as I could no longer tolerate his behaviour. I gave the ring back and told him that I felt he had serious problems and that he needed help. I finally told my family what was going on (which was really embarrassing), and they supported my decision to break it off. He did not like this and couldn't accept that I was ending things with him. He tried to involve my sister to get her to influence my decision and change my mind. Obviously, that plan backfired for him, but he could not believe that I was actually ending it.

That's not so bad, right? I got out of a bad situation before it was "too late," didn't I? Unfortunately, I did not. In the beginning, I did keep to my word and I did not get back together with him, and I left every weekend to visit friends in other cities so that I could get some distance since we lived in the same house. I even dated someone else for a while, which was really good for me. However, at Christmas that year, when I was at home with my family, he showed up to my parents' house with a very thoughtful gift that he made chronicling our time together, and he put on an amazing heartfelt performance in front of my entire family. He talked about how he had gone to therapy, that he had done a lot of work to change his habits, that he could not imagine a life without me, and on and on. There were tears, and he succeeded in winning me over with this grand gesture, and, perhaps more importantly to him, winning my family over as well. So, we got back together. A couple of months later, he proposed to me again on my birthday, in front of my family. I finished my final year of school and he was accepted into a master's program back in Nova Scotia, so I moved back with him to begin teaching in Halifax despite being offered my dream job in Ontario. We got married the following year, even though there were still some red flags (like him refusing to take care of me after my tonsil surgery a few months before the wedding- my parents had to come up to stay with me for two weeks because *his* routine and schedule could not be disrupted).

We bought a house because *he* decided we should, even though he contributed nothing to the down payment. I had the car, I paid for the mortgage of the house, I helped him with his medical school application, and I also spent a great deal of time and effort to help him get into the Medical Officer Training Program (MOTP) through various influential connections that I had at that time, to which he was accepted halfway through his medical school studies. This allowed for the rest of his schooling to be paid for, as well as a guaranteed job with the military for five years. He continued to over-extend himself by playing on various sports teams, coaching, and doing things to help out our friends. Everyone always said that he was "the best" and that I was "so lucky" to have him. There were many times when I wanted to respond to these comments with, "Yes, he is great to everyone else, but you don't have to go home with him."

Although I believe he stopped cheating on me (and he was much more covert with his porn habit), his subtle manipulation and emotional abuse continued. I didn't recognize it or understand that it was not okay until some close friends started witnessing the things that he did: getting angry when I asked him what he wanted for supper, tossing aside a gift I brought home for him without thanking me, taking a cab home and leaving me alone downtown in a snowstorm because he was mad at me for crying and being upset that my winter jacket had gotten lost in a coat check (apparently, I "embarrassed" him). In each of these instances, it was me that ended up apologizing. He was so good at twisting things around to make me feel guilty and make me think that I had things wrong-that *I* was the problem and not him.

My friends started to point out that the way he was treating me was not acceptable. I defended him because I had become so brainwashed that he was right and I was always wrong. However, the more they pointed things out to me, the more I began to question whether they might be right. I mean, I definitely knew that the anger outbursts were not okay. Ripping his clothing into shreds with his hands while yelling at me, throwing a hockey stick down the hall at me, purposefully smashing and breaking things that meant a lot to me, punching things around me, grabbing my shoulders and shaking me ... I knew that his temper was bad.

It wasn't until he began threatening to leave me again (which he used to do in the early years of our relationship, when things didn't go his way. He would start packing bags and I would beg him to stop, and then I would give in to whatever it was that he wanted so that he wouldn't leave) that I really started to understand that I was being manipulated and controlled. He told me that I needed to get on board with having kids according to *his* timeline and grand life schedule that he mapped out for his life (which he neglected to share with me). If I didn't agree to start having kids ASAP, then he would leave. I was certainly not a relationship expert, but I knew enough to listen to my gut and not give in to this threat. Something about having a kid because I was forced to do so according to someone else's timeline did not sit well with me (hmm... I can't imagine why).

I said no to this, which, of course, he could not accept, so he got my parents and sister involved so that they would start tag-teaming me about getting on board and starting a family. I had not told them about any of the other things that had been going on since we got back together, because I needed some element of peace in my life. Worrying about my family hating him (again) was not something I had the capacity for, so I kept it all to myself. Naturally, when he phoned them up to tell them how unreasonable I was, they believed him and supported him. He had them wrapped around his finger and he knew it.

When I continued to resist, things got ugly really fast. In a dark moment of despair, one night after a few drinks, I ended up kissing a male friend who I confided in about what was going on. It was a low point for me, and obviously not a good decision, and it is a moment that I still regret. However, when Mike found out about it, he went ballistic (and conveniently dismissed any of the previous cheating and full-on secret relationships that he had with other women while we were dating). I felt incredibly guilty, because *I* did this when we were *married*. He secretly called my family, who were all in Florida at the time, and told them that I had gone crazy, that I was cheating on him with multiple men, that he had proof, and that I needed psychiatric help. Of course, my family had no idea that what he was saying were lies and manipulation, so they were all beside themselves thinking that I had had a nervous breakdown. My mother and my sister wouldn't talk to me, and my dad told me that I had to get serious help and be a better wife. I had no idea where this was coming from, or what Mike had said to them- in my head, this was all because of the kiss. Meanwhile, they thought that I had lost my mind and was now a cheating nymphomaniac.

This was the lowest point of my life - the absolute rock bottom. From what I knew, my family alienated me because I did this *terrible* thing, and now I had to atone for my huge sin. I started going to therapy on my own, and I suggested that we go to couple's counselling, where he attempted to shame me to the therapist. Thankfully, she did not buy into it. We attended a few sessions and things got marginally better, but in our final session, she asked to speak to me privately. She told me that I had to end the relationship because it wasn't good for me and I needed to find a healthier path. I was shocked by her bluntness and grateful for it too, because I knew she was right.

When I called my family that day, my sister finally agreed to talk to me, and I told her about all of the things that were going on, what I did, and that I felt really terrible. She didn't know what I was talking about. She then told me the story that she and my parents were given, which was so unbelievably horrifying. This was the ultimate manipulation and betrayal. I was *so* angry and confused by how Mike could do such a thing. My poor family felt terrible too, especially my mother, because they believed him without talking to me. I knew they had no reason not to believe him. I was trying to keep the peace between everyone; because of that, they had no idea about the things that were happening. I don't blame them at all for believing him - he was always a master at manipulating and lying since he was in junior high. I was just so thankful that everything was now out in the open and that everything now made sense.

Within a day, I packed up some bags, told him I was leaving, and said I wanted a divorce. I went to stay with a close friend and work colleague of mine, who so generously allowed me to stay with her and her husband for a couple of months until I figured out my next steps. He was in shock that I left. The crazy thing is, even after all that, *I still felt guilty* for leaving. I let him use my car until he could get one so that he could get to school easily. I separated our things thoughtfully and carefully, making sure to be fair. He demanded to keep the house, and I didn't argue - I didn't want to be there anyway. He also wanted both of our dogs, and I didn't want to split them up, so I agreed. I knew that there would be some kind of punishment, though (as there always was), for embarrassing him and leaving him. Sure enough, he used the fact that I helped him to get a student line of credit for his on-going studies to his advantage. Since I co-signed for it (he couldn't get it on his own) and we were married, I was legally on the hook for half of it, and he pushed to make me take on the full half, which I fought. In the end, I still ended up with a third of his debt because I didn't have money to pay all these legal fees. It took the next five years to pay off. This could have easily become something for me to be bitter about for a long time, but I chose to think of it as the cost of my freedom. Thinking about what my freedom was worth made it much easier to swallow and a much more positive way to look at it.

So, that's how eight years of emotional, mental, and verbal abuse (with some physical aggression) ended for me. I was pretty much a complete wreck, and the anxiety that I felt at times was paralyzing. Luckily, I had an *amazing* therapist who helped me to see all of the false beliefs that I had about myself and my worthiness. She helped me see the extent of the manipulation and that I was the victim of gaslighting for many years. She taught me about narcissistic personality traits and narcissistic abuse, and that was exactly what I lived through. I continued therapy for several months until I moved to the Dominican Republic (more on this later). My family was incredibly supportive during the whole process. I don't think they will ever be able to forgive Mike for how he treated them, and my poor mother still feels guilty for abandoning me in those weeks, even though I have told her many times that I do not hold that against her. She was manipulated by him, as I was for so many years. Things were changing for the better, and I knew that, but there were those dark and lonely moments, lying in bed at night, where I just felt so incredibly *lost* and alone - just like Chuck Noland on that raft. I didn't know who I was anymore, but I knew I had to find out.

Since then, I have done a *lot* of personal growth work. Through being temporarily homeless and staying at friends' houses, moving to a developing country, being single for a year, getting involved in new activities, meeting new people, and being open to new experiences, I rediscovered myself over those first two years living on my own. I reconnected with my previous passions that were long forgotten when I was consumed by my ex's needs and making him happy. I also learned and recognized that I played a role in what happened because I tolerated his disrespect. I was *not* a victim - I was an enabler. When I finally got back into dating, I did it in slow motion. My next relationship was mostly over long distance for the first six months.

After moving back to Canada, I switched schools to have a fresh start teaching with different people, and I decided to go back to school and get my master's in counselling psychology. I realized that helping other people through their most difficult times was a passion and a calling for me. Going through that master's program was another process of significant personal growth for me, and it was also the first time that I ever shared this part of my life with other people. As it turned out, many other women resonated with my story, as they have also lived through toxic relationship experiences. Since I started my career as a therapist, helping women as they navigate through the end of their own toxic intimate relationships and begin a new life is a cornerstone of my work, and I feel truly grateful that I am able to turn my pain into something positive that, hopefully, helps others to live better lives too.

Chapter 3:
SO ... NOW WHAT?

To create a new life for myself as "Heather 2.0," there was a lot of personal growth work that I had to do, as I mentioned. You may be wondering what that means, or what it looks like. Of course, each person's personal growth journey looks different, but there are some basic guidelines and concepts that are pretty universal when engaging in this kind of work. In this book, I've broken down this work into specific steps to help guide you through this process, based on my own personal experience and on some of my clinical work with clients in similar situations. When you're on that raft in the middle of the ocean, I've learned that there's not much you can do other than use the skills and knowledge that you have to navigate to your next destination - wherever that may be - as best as you can. Think of this book as your step-by-step "emergency first aid survival guide" for recovering from a toxic relationship and learning to live independently.

This is Your Roadmap

I've created this as a roadmap to a fresh start and a new outlook on life, leaving the old life in the past and moving forward towards a hopeful future filled with possibilities and new opportunities. We're going to begin, in the next chapter, with where you are stuck - in your old holding patterns and ways of thinking that are not serving you. We are going to take a look at what's holding you back from moving forward and how to let go of those things. We're also going to examine those intrusive thoughts that keep you up at night and keep you feeling anxious all day long. We're going to talk about how to *stop* them from happening and replace them with calmer, more reasonable thoughts. In Chapter 6, we're going to take a look at your fears and understand what fear is in general, so that you can overcome the fears that are preventing you from living your best life possible.

Understanding your emotions is another area we are going to look at (in Chapter 8), and how to take control of your feelings, rather than allow them to control you and your decisions. Once we work on banishing your fears and controlling your emotions, there will be room for you to start figuring out what makes you *happy* and focus on bringing more of those things into your life. "Finding your happy" is one of my favourite things to work on (cue Pharrell's "Happy" song… one of my favourites!), and it is a crucial component to this whole "starting your life over" thing that we are doing. Let's face it, if you're not happy in what you're doing, it defeats the whole purpose of living independently on your own. Make sense?

Building a network of support is also a key part of being on your own, so we are going to spend some time in Chapter 9 talking about supports you already have in place and how to connect with new people so that you can create a solid network of people that you trust that is uniquely yours and that you can rely on to help you when you need it (and no, I am not talking about getting more Instagram followers). Finally, we are going to talk about *confidence* and how to get it back: self-esteem, self-worth, self-talk, self-love - all of the things that we need to increase to build up our confidence. This also includes learning how to stand up for yourself and to not be afraid to use your voice… because (that's right!) you're *worth it*.

A Source of Reference

This is a book that you can come back to again and again, as much as you need to, whenever you feel like you're stuck on that life raft all by yourself. There may be specific chapters or sections that you want to revisit from time to time, and I hope that you do. For your first time through, however, I've set the book up in a specific order on purpose as building blocks to use on your path to creating your new life. Based on my own learning and experience, both personally and professionally, I have designed this in a way that I hope will make the most sense to you and bring the most relief to you as quickly as possible. Once you've got a handle on starting to recover emotionally, mentally, and physically, we will move on to the more concrete growth work that I mentioned above, in a logical order that (I hope) feels manageable for you. I designed this book in this way specifically so that you do not feel overwhelmed when you're most likely already feeling overwhelmed. Each step is covered in its own chapter, and each step is broken down into smaller parts with specific ideas, tips, examples, and strategies of how to implement them. The ideas that I share for taking action and implementation are by no means exhaustive, and I encourage you to incorporate your own ideas in each step, as they make the most sense for you, your life, and your situation.

By the time you get to the end of this book, you will have essentially completed a crash course on how to start your life over after ending a toxic relationship and how to live your new life independently, happily, healthily, and with purpose. You will have all the tools you need to navigate your life raft from the middle of that vast ocean towards a destination of your choosing. There will still be waves and stormy seas at times, but when they hit, you'll know how to navigate them and get back on course while staying true to yourself and your purpose. Tools for your life of independence, strength, and happiness - that is what I'm giving to you in this book. Are you ready? Let's get started.

Chapter 4:

ROADBLOCKS

To move forward with your new life, we first have to figure out what may be getting in the way. I like to think of these things as roadblocks, because once we come upon them, we then have to come up with a plan of how to navigate through or around them so that we can keep going. In my own experience, I struggled with several roadblocks, including pride, fear, holding onto the hurt, and second-guessing my decision to leave. Through my clinical work, I discovered that many other women are also struggling with the same things as they navigate their way to starting the next phase of their lives (no, I wasn't the only one). Given how common these roadblocks seem to be for women, I thought it would be a good idea to talk about each of them on their own.

Pride

Let's start with pride. Pride is that feeling of deep pleasure or satisfaction that we get from achieving something that is admired by other people. For example, when we are young and we win a contest or a race, or we get a medal or a certificate, there is usually a crowd of people clapping and cheering. This makes us feel proud. Maybe there was that hard exam that we aced, that elite school we got into, or that incredible job that we were offered. All these things are tied to our pride. They are achievements that are recognized and celebrated by others. Don't get me wrong, these are all positive things that we should feel proud of, as they are often the result of hard work and dedication. However, pride can become problematic when the thing that we worked really hard for doesn't work out. Maybe you didn't get the job offer even though you had a great interview and made it to the final rounds of the hiring process. Maybe you didn't finish that Ironman race due to an injury that happened at mile twenty-three of your run (to any of you who even sign up for those things… you are my hero). You worked hard to accomplish those goals, but it didn't turn out the way you thought or hoped that it would.

Our pride prevents us from picking up and carrying on to the next opportunity. We may start thinking things like, "What was wrong with me? How am I going to tell everyone that I didn't get the job?" or, "I can't show my face in my running group ever again because I am a disgrace and a failure." Why do we tend to say these things to ourselves? Because our pride is attached to our ego, and when our ego gets bruised, it gets in the way of seeing things objectively and clearly. The same is true when we decide to end a relationship that we know, deep down, is bad for us. Over time, it became unhealthy and toxic, and there is no way to recover from it other than to leave. Yet, even though we know this is true (with every fibre of our being), we feel a deep sense of shame when there is nothing to be ashamed about. We tried our hardest and gave our best effort, but it didn't work out... and that's okay. But our pride doesn't let us feel like it's okay. Our bruised egos convince us that we are somehow not good enough, and we feel embarrassed to show our faces to the world.

Ego and Fear

As if that were not bad enough, our pride and ego are also the sources of the fears that we have about moving forward. You may be wondering, "What is this ego thing, anyway? I've heard of it before, but I don't really know what it is or how it affects me." Here's the CliffsNotes version. The ego is that part of the self that is attached to our response to perceived danger. This dates all the way back to our more primitive periods in history, when the risk of being chased and attacked by a saber-tooth tiger was a legitimate problem. We had this built-in response to danger (the "oh crap, that tiger is coming towards me" kind of danger), where we did one of three things: fight the tiger, run away, or freeze and do nothing. The ego, at that time, was that voice that told us to be careful, that maybe we shouldn't leave the cave in case there is a tiger out there. It was the voice that tried to protect us from real possible danger. Unfortunately, this part of our psyche hasn't evolved that much over time. We still have that same "fight, flight, or freeze" response to situations that we perceive to be dangerous, even though there are no longer saber-tooth tigers chasing us. Thousands of years later, our bodies still react in the same way when we feel like something scary is somehow threatening, and our ego voices say things to try to "keep us safe" from things that could be "dangerous" (i.e., anything that is new. New equals unknown, and unknown equals danger). So, it seems that our brains are naturally programmed to keep us from doing anything new because it could be "dangerous." Our egos exist for the sole purpose of protecting us from perceived danger, so it talks us out of doing things that are good for us and instead talks us into believing that what we want to do is bad, scary, or wrong.

So, how does this show up as a roadblock to moving forward with your life? Often, after deciding to end a toxic relationship, the ego voice grabs a megaphone and yells, "But what will everyone think of us? What will they say?

They are going to judge us for doing this." Yup, the good, old, reliable fear of judgment shows up. What *will* people think? What *will* they say? How can you possibly move forward with everyone talking about you? These thoughts can be crippling to any attempts at moving on with our lives. We can become very consumed with doing things according to what we think *other people* might think - so much so that it sometimes leads us to completely withdraw from family and friends. Think about that for a minute. We let the fear of judgement from other people (who, by the way, have no idea what it has been like living in your shoes) dictate what we do - or, more appropriately, what we *don't* do. Now, if you were to listen to a friend who came and shared these exact thoughts with you, what would you tell this friend? My guess is it would be something along the lines of, "Who cares what other people think about you? Their opinions don't matter. You have to do what is best for *you*. People who are judging you are a bunch of busybodies anyway - what do they know? You can't let the possible opinions of a bunch of gossip queens dictate your life." Does that sound about right? I thought so…. Isn't it interesting how much easier it is for us to give our family and friends this dose of truth and reality, yet we somehow are unable to do this for ourselves? Thanks, ego, you're *so* (not) helpful.

Second-Guessing Your Decision

Now that we have established a solid foundation of ego-driven roadblocks of pride and fear of judgement for what we are doing, it's time to add in a double shot of second-guessing our decision to leave. Oh yes, the all-familiar "Oh no - what the heck am I doing? This was a huge mistake and I am crazy" train. Now that you've actually left the toxic relationship that you were in (for however long), the ego's "danger" sensor is in overdrive and is sounding the alarms whenever possible. Remember, this is because it is trying to protect us from being eaten by tigers…. If we stay in "the cave" (i.e., any situation where things are the same, familiar, and more comfortable than the unknown), then we know what will happen in there and we won't be in any *new* danger. The tigers can't get into the cave, so we better run as fast as we can and dive back in. This is the only way to make this feeling of panic go away, right? *Wrong!* I know that it really *feels* that way. There is so much to figure out and get used to, and it is so over-stimulating and feels overwhelming, and going back to the situation that we know feels like it would be so much easier… but this is absolutely untrue. Going back to the toxic relationship patterns of the cycle of abuse is the worst thing that we could possibly do. "But Heather, what about this horrible feeling?" Short answer - this panic feeling is not based on facts. It's based on our unsubstantiated fears, but I'll get more into this later. What is important to know right now is that the flip-flopping back and forth on the decision you made to leave the relationship that was no longer serving you is a huge roadblock to moving forward with finding your independence in your new life.

Holding on to the Hurt

The last big thing that tends to get in the way of moving on and healing is our tendency to hold on to the hurt that we feel. All that pain and suffering - the emotional, verbal, and/or physical abuse that we may have endured, the fighting, the resentments, *all* of the things that have deeply hurt us over the years, and ultimately led to our decision to end the relationship and leave. I am not saying that these feelings of hurt are not valid or important to work through. In fact, I argue that working through the hurt and healing those wounds is the most important work that you ever do, and it is necessary to fully move on and be happy. What I am saying is that it can be easy to get stuck in those feelings of hurt and focus on all the injustices that happened in the relationship. This is perhaps the biggest roadblock of all, because it can become all-consuming and, if we are not careful, over time it can become an impermeable wall of bitterness, contempt, and a sense of being perpetually wronged by the world. Getting caught up in the thought of not deserving the suffering that you endured becomes toxic and poisonous to all relationships - not just intimate relationships. Of course, you didn't deserve to be treated poorly, abused, taken advantage of, manipulated, or any other of the horrible things that you went through in your toxic relationship, but it's not about *deserving*. The unfortunate part of living in this world is that, sometimes, bad things happen for no reason that we can possibly understand.

Our need to attach blame or come up with reasons for why something horrible happened is an entirely futile effort. Why did Hitler murder 11 million people? Why did Stalin conduct his murderous purges? Why is there hunger, water-born diseases, and constant rape and pillaging of women in villages in underdeveloped countries? The answers to these atrocities are so complex that they are beyond our ability to truly accurately explain or comprehend. The truth is, no one deserves these horrible things that happen to them. The sad reality is that there is no one explanation or reason why people behave in these horrific ways towards their fellow human beings. If we focus on this idea of being wronged for too long, our minds can easily become entrenched in the poison of our hurt, which negatively impacts us for the rest of our lives. I really do not want this to be your fate, so it will be vitally important for us to work on redirecting your focus away from, "Why did this happen to me?" and turn it towards putting our energy into our own recovery, healing, and self-care.

Chapter 5:

TAKING CARE OF YOURSELF
(AND WHY IT MATTERS)

One of the first things that I focus on with people when they first come to see me is self-care. You've probably heard a lot about the importance of self-care recently (which is fantastic). Maybe you've heard celebrities talk about it about in the media, or maybe it's a new organizational initiative that has been brought into your workplace. But what does it mean, exactly? If you were to search the meaning of self-care, this is what comes up. "The practice of taking an active role in protecting one's own well-being and happiness, particularly during periods of stress." In other words, self-care is any activity that we do *on purpose* to take care of our mental, emotional, and physical health. When we are faced with significant distress in our lives (say, for example, leaving a toxic relationship and starting a new life), these are the times when self-care is the *most* important. I will be totally honest with you here. After I decided to end my toxic relationship, and after I left, I was an absolute emotional and physical wreck. My tank was below empty and I was running on fumes. My sleep was pretty much non-existent, I had no appetite, and I still had to go to work and show up for my students in a very challenging school environment every day. I lost ten pounds without trying, as I felt too stressed and overwhelmed to eat. Just making the decision to leave and then actually leaving, took such a significant toll on my mental, emotional, and physical well-being. I was a mess, and my therapist at the time can totally attest to that. Believe me when I tell you that *I get it*.

It was in therapy where I learned that I needed to start taking care of myself, but I was so depleted at that time that I didn't know what that meant or where to begin. Maybe you're feeling the same way. So, let's explore this together. How do you know what kind of self-care you need? One way to help you to focus in on the aspects of taking care of yourself that may be missing is to complete a self-care questionnaire (kind of like those Cosmo quizzes you used to do in high school, only this is focused on *you* instead of "how to get that guy to be into you" - insert eye-roll here. Quick answer, Cosmo. You don't). To help you with this, I've included a sample questionnaire at the back of this book created by the Institute for Functional

Medicine - feel free to use it or search for another one that you feel would be most helpful. The benefit of completing a self-care survey is that it makes it really easy to see the things that we are already doing to take care of ourselves, and it shows us the big gaps where we need to turn our focus. Most questionnaires examine different categories of our well-being: physical, emotional/spiritual, professional work/career, social life/family/relationships, and balance.

Types of Self-Care

So, what does self-care look like? It looks like all of those items listed in the questionnaire you filled out. Let's look at some examples of self-care activities in the most common categories:

1. Physical: healthy/regular eating, exercise, getting enough sleep, medical care, time off

2. Psychological: journal writing, personal psycho-therapy, self-help reading, self-reflection

3. Emotional/Spiritual: participating in activities you enjoy, expressing feelings (e.g., crying), positive affirmations, spending time in nature, meditating/praying, singing

4. Professional/Career: taking breaks, setting limits, chatting with co-workers, balancing workload, negotiating for your needs

5. Social/Family: spending time with people close to you, asking for help, engaging with a supportive network (friends/family members)

Hopefully, you're starting to see a clearer picture of what taking care of yourself looks like. Now, imagine that we are sitting together in our very first session, and I have asked you the following questions: How are you sleeping? What are you eating these days? How often are you able to exercise? What kinds of things are you doing to relax? Write down your answers to these questions (yes, really - go grab a pen and paper and jot down your answers!). If you are currently in a state that is anywhere close to mine when I first left my relationship, the answers to these are likely not stellar - and that's okay! We are going to get you on a healthier track and feeling better, starting *right now*.

Sleep Matters

First up: sleep. Why is sleep so important? According to the Mental Health Foundation, sleep is as important to our health as eating, drinking, and breathing. It allows our bodies to repair themselves and our brains to consolidate our memories and process information. It's important because our brains and bodies need it to be able to rebuild, rejuvenate, and heal. It also allows us to think more clearly when we are awake, increases our tolerance levels of distress, and decreases symptoms of anxiety and depression. Poor sleep is the number one complaint that I get from my clients when they first come to see me, so I like to engage in an exploration of sleep habits: What time to do go to bed? Do you go to bed and wake up at the same time each day? What are you doing an hour before you go to bed (i.e., are you looking at a TV screen/tablet/phone)? What is your "get ready for bed" routine? Are you eating/drinking alcohol/smoking/consuming recreational drugs before bed? Write down your answers. Here are the basic rules that I recommend for creating a healthy sleep routine that will get you back to feeling more rested:

1. Decide on a set time to go to bed and wake up each day, if you can (I know this can be a challenge for rotating shift workers).

2. Turn off the screens at least one hour before going to bed. Yes, I am 100 percent serious - the data is in and says screens are bad for your sleep, so stop looking at them an hour before bed.

3. Develop a routine before going to bed: take a bath or a long hot shower, listen to relaxing music,

make some "sleepy time" tea, read a book (an actual book with pages).

4. Start listening to guided meditations for sleep each night; this helps your brain to focus on something else other than your racing thoughts, to-do lists, and worries. Look up "The Honest Guys" and check out the playlists on their YouTube channel. They have a whole playlist of sleep meditations. Or, download the "Insight Timer" app and search for sleep meditations with specific filters (time limit, topic, male/female voice, etc.).

5. Avoid recreational drugs, alcohol, and nicotine. All of these things interfere with the body's ability to have restful deep sleep (which is what our bodies and brains need).

6. Create a relaxing space for sleep. Take the TV out of the bedroom (I mean it - this is huge), get a lamp or two with lower wattage light bulbs, or diffuse some lavender essential oil if you enjoy essential oils.

7. Consider taking a melatonin supplement for a couple of weeks to help your body's natural cadence to get back on track (this is especially helpful for

shift workers). Talk to a pharmacist about the best kind to get (I find the kind that dissolves under your tongue to be most effective).

You don't have to make all these changes all at once if you feel like it's too drastic. Instead, start implementing them one at a time, adding another one each week to see how your quality of sleep changes over that period.

Fuelling Your Body and Mind

Now that we've got a plan to get your sleep under control, I want to talk about eating. Food is important. Just like your body requires sleep to function, it also requires "fuel." Our fuel comes in the form of food. Whole foods, natural vitamin and mineral supplements, and plenty of water is the recipe for a well-functioning body and mind. Think of it as "premium" fuel for your body, similar to what you'd put in a fancy high-end car. Our bodies are not that different from cars. The types of fuel that we put into our bodies makes all the difference. What we eat directly affects the structure and function of our brain and, ultimately, our mood. Just like that expensive car, our brain functions best when it gets only premium fuel. Eating high-quality foods that contain lots of vitamins, minerals, and antioxidants nourish the brain and protect it from cell damage. Unfortunately, just like an expensive car, your brain can be damaged if you take in anything other than premium fuel. If substances from "low-premium" fuel (like what you get from fast, processed, or refined foods) get to the brain, it has little ability to get rid of them. Diets high in refined sugars, for example, are harmful to the brain. Multiple studies have found a correlation between a diet high in refined sugars and impaired brain function, and even a worsening of symptoms of mood disorders such as depression.

Ladies, food *does* matter, and we need it for our bodies to run. If we don't fuel it at all, it will stop working. If we fuel it with garbage, it will stop working, plain and simple. If you're finding it hard to force yourself to eat right now, I recommend trying something that is easy for your body to digest: fruit and greens smoothies, egg whites (I like to add a little cinnamon to make it taste more like French Toast), or full, balanced, ready-made meal replacement supplements (meaning forty percent protein, thirty percent carbs, and thirty percent healthy fats) are all good options for getting that premium fuel into your body with minimum effort to prepare it or for your body to process it. I love whole foods and I love to cook, but we can't get everything we need just from our whole foods, and sometimes our lives are too overwhelming to even think about cooking. I am a big proponent of natural supplementation products that fill in those gaps and make it as easy as possible to get quality nutrition into my body. Visiting a registered dietician or nutritionist might be the best way for you to get some ideas of what would work best for your lifestyle.

Time to Sweat

Exercise is also *really* important in times of high stress, transition, and turmoil. I am not expecting or asking you to start training for a marathon tomorrow. What I am asking you to do is look at simple ways that you can increase exercise into your day. Can you park farther away from the door of the building you need to go into? Can you walk or bike places to run some of your errands? Can you go for a fifteen-minute walk during a break in your workday? I'm pretty sure the answer to most of these questions is "yes," so the real question is, what is getting in the way of doing these things? Once you answer that question, think about ways you can problem-solve so that you can start to do these things. Or, maybe you already do them (way to go!) and you need to up your intensity level.

Why is this exercise thing such a big deal? Well, as Elle Woods once said, "Exercise releases endorphins. Endorphins make you happy. Happy people don't kill their husbands - they just don't!" Okay, *Legally Blonde* joking aside, Elle Woods was actually right. Exercise makes us feel good because it releases chemicals like endorphins and serotonin that improve our mood. Health Direct (a Department of Health agency in Australia) reports that if you exercise regularly, it can reduce your stress and symptoms of mental health conditions like depression and anxiety and help with recovery from mental health issues. It also helps improve your sleep (so let's add that to our sleep routine list), which is important for the reasons we already discussed. Exercise also helps our mind. It pumps blood to the brain, which helps us to think more clearly. It also increases the size of the hippocampus, the part of the brain responsible for memory.

"OK, I'm in. But how much exercise do I need?" Research shows that three or more sessions per week of aerobic exercise (walking, cycling, swimming, running) or resistance training (weight lifting, bodyweight exercise) for forty-five to sixty minutes per session can help treat even chronic depression. Effects are noticeable after about four weeks of regular exercise three times a week. Exercise levels below these recommended amounts are still beneficial, and, of course, the side effects (weight loss, increased energy, better skin, improved physical health, etc.) are fantastic too. So, go grab your schedule/planner and block in three exercise sessions for this coming week. It needs to be scheduled as a non-negotiable appointment, like going to the doctor or the dentist. Otherwise, you are more likely to "not get to it." Keep track of the things you are doing so you can see your progress over the next few weeks.

Back to Your Results

Now that we've covered the "big three" musts for psychical self-care, it's time to go back to your questionnaire results. Where do you need to focus your efforts the most (i.e., in which areas are you suffering the most)? Emotional/mental self-care? Social/family? Professional/career? Take a look, and focus on *one thing* that you can do in each area where you are suffering. Do not try to do a bunch of things all at once. You will only end up feeling overwhelmed and over-scheduled (which is totally counter-productive to the goal of self-care). I would like to end this section by quickly highlighting a few other key self-care practices that I found to be most helpful both for my clients and for myself.

1. Practice gratitude. Gratitude improves our psychological health, as it reduces a multitude of toxic emotions, ranging from envy and resentment to frustration and regret - feelings that can be (for me, at least) prominent in this time of transition and leaving a toxic relationship. Robert A. Emmons, Ph. D., a leading gratitude researcher, conducted multiple studies on the link between gratitude and well-being. His research supports that gratitude effectively increases happiness and reduces depression.

2. Take a vacation. If it is at all possible for you to take some time off from work - whether it be stress leave, vacation days, or personal days - do *it*. Do not come up with a list of excuses why you can't. I promise you, in ninety-nine percent of cases, you can. Someone can look after your kids for a few days, someone can take care of your dog, and someone can pick up the slack for you at work. It's possible, and I argue that it is necessary in your process of healing and taking your next steps into the world - just get away from everything and everyone, even if it's just for a couple of days. If finances are a concern, maybe you can borrow a friend's tent and go camping for a few days. If the idea of camping makes you want to vomit (like it does for my sister), ask a friend or an extended family member if you can escape to their cottage or trailer for a couple of days, or start a GoFundMe campaign to raise a couple of hundred dollars for an Airbnb. Cash in those Air Miles and book a flight. I don't care what it is or how it looks - just find a way to make it happen! Allina Health explains why taking a vacation is so important.

Improved mental health. Neuroscientists found that brain structure is altered by chronic exposure to the stress hormone cortisol, which can be a major contributing factor to anxiety and depression. Feelings of calm arise from time away from work and relieve stress, which allows the body and mind to heal in ways that it couldn't if it were still under pressure.

- Greater well-being. According to a Gallup study, people who "always make time for regular trips" had a 68.4 score on the Gallup-Heathway's Well-Being Index, in comparison to a 51.4 well-being score for less frequent travellers. One study found that three days after vacation, subjects' physical complaints, quality of sleep, and mood improved when compared to before vacation. These gains were still present five weeks later, especially in those who had more personal time and overall satisfaction during their vacation.

- Increased mental power. Upon returning from vacation, workers are often more focused and productive. Studies found that chronic stress can actually modulate a part of the brain that inhibits goal-directed activity and can cause problems with memory. Time off can tune up a well-functioning brain.

- Decreased burnout. Workers who take regular time to relax are less likely to experience burnout, making them more creative and productive than their overworked, under-rested counterparts.

- Planning the trip boosts happiness. Research shows the biggest boost in happiness comes from planning the vacation. A person can feel the effects up to eight weeks before the trip!

  The bottom line is, taking time away from the stresses of work and daily life can improve our health, motivation, relationships, job performance, and perspective, and give us the break we need to return to our lives and jobs refreshed and better equipped to handle whatever comes.

3. Do more "feel good" activities. For me this looks like taking a bath, reading light books, getting a massage, and rocking out to some empowering music (Madonna and Lady Gaga, anyone?). Whatever just makes you feel fantastic, do it!

4. Get a pet. This may not be possible for everyone, but it might be for some of you. Personally, I have no idea how I would have survived the heartaches of my life without a dog. Now, I realize that you may not be in a position to go adopt a dog, cat, or bird, but you may be able to borrow someone else's pet from

time to time, which will also have massively positive benefits for your mental well-being.

5. Explore possible medication with a doctor. Sometimes, no matter what we do, we are still really struggling with regulating ourselves. The overwhelming feelings are still there and the life-sucking depression is still weighing you down even though you are making positive changes. Your brain just may be unable to fire between synapses properly right now, either due to the stress that you are currently feeling, the psychological distress you endured during the time you were in your toxic relationship, or a variety of other factors. In these situations, I almost always encourage my clients to go and talk to a physician about the possibility of requiring prescription medication. I had to do this for myself, and I am not ashamed to share this with you. I recognized that I was really not doing well and that I needed to "double down" on my treatment from both the medical and the therapy side of things in order to get back to feeling like myself. This is no different than a person requiring insulin, blood pressure medication, or prescription sunglasses.

When our organs stop working properly, sometimes we need to make a medical correction.

Ladies, our brains are the most important organs that we have besides our hearts, and without it, nothing else in our bodies works. So, if you wouldn't refuse to take insulin because your pancreas stopped working due to factors outside of your control (i.e., you have a healthy lifestyle), or if you wouldn't refuse to take medication to help your blood pressure, why would we refuse to take medication to help our brains to fire properly? It doesn't make sense. I am not saying that everyone should start popping pills because they are stressed or sad. What I am saying is that, sometimes, the chemical reactions in our brains get messed up, and we need to explore our options of what might best bring that into balance. I am *not* a doctor, so my advice to you is go talk to one if you think that medication might be a good option *for you.*

A Final Word on Self-Care

Be gentle with yourself. Be kind, compassionate, and understanding of yourself. If thinking about doing this is hard for you, try thinking about how you would treat a close friend who was going through your situation. What would you do for her? What words would you share with her? How would you support her? Write down your answers to these questions and then look at them. *That* is how you need to talk to yourself and treat yourself.

No "yes, but" or "that's different." You are deserving and you are worthy. Be kind to yourself the way you would be kind to a dear friend. This is the best way you can take care of yourself. Learning how to do this and giving yourself permission to engage in self-care is *non-negotiable*, especially as we begin to work through letting go of the lies that are holding us back.

Chapter 6:

THE LIES WE BELIEVE

Now that we identified the roadblocks that we create and put up (which we talked about in Chapter 4), it is important to recognize the lies that we tell ourselves that keep us from moving past these roadblocks. No, this is not a spin-off from *Girl, Wash Your Face* by Rachel Hollis (but if you have not read it, I highly recommend it - it is so helpful in identifying the lies that we, as women, believe about ourselves in all of the other aspects of our lives). However, creating an awareness of these false beliefs (the lies) that are not serving you is a crucial step moving forward and becoming fully independent and confident living on your own. Many of us have a habit of living in the same narrative that we were stuck in during the time of our toxic relationship, but this narrative is something we created and told to ourselves *back then,* when we were in that horrible situation. Now that we have made the courageous decision to leave that relationship behind, we must also leave that old narrative behind with it.

What They Sound Like

So, let's get into it. What are the lies that we tell ourselves? Well, they could be all sorts of things. I remember one of the biggest false beliefs that I had after I finally made the decision and ended my toxic relationship was that I wasn't strong enough to stick to my decision and be on my own. I convinced myself that it was just too hard, that I would never get back on my feet because the debt was so far over my head. I thought that I was not smart enough to be able to figure things out (e.g., how could I fix something in the house if it broke? I didn't know how to use power tools, let alone own any). My ego voice was working overtime in protection mode, and it was very good at convincing me that these things were true, especially in the first few weeks. Then, there was the guilt - the soul-sucking, gut-wrenching guilt over leaving my partner. I became fixated on the idea that I was a bad person because I left my partner and I was not honouring the commitment that I made to him. I felt incredibly guilty for hurting him even though he hurt me and manipulated me repeatedly for years. This guilt then spiralled into thinking that I deserved to be miserable and that I made a huge mess of my life.

Now, of course, I cannot forget about all of the mothers out there. That's right - enter the "mom guilt." Deciding to end the relationship with your child's other legal parent can bring on a whole tidal wave of mom guilt. At this point, I must share with you my favourite quote from Rachel Hollis in her latest book. "Mom guilt is garbage!" Yup, it sure is. It is completely unhelpful and a guilt-inducing phenomenon that chisels away at your soul. Nonetheless, it seems that moms are unable to get away from the guilt that surrounds the decision of leaving your partner when children are involved: "Am I ruining my child's life by breaking up the family? Am I messing my kid up permanently because of this? Am I selfish and a bad mom because I had to leave?" Do any of these things sound familiar to you?

Cognitive Distortions

All these lies (some of which I fully believed) are called cognitive distortions - ways that our mind convinces us of something that isn't true. These inaccurate thoughts are usually used to reinforce negative thinking or emotions. We tell ourselves things that we think sound rational and accurate, but they only serve to keep us feeling bad about ourselves. We can also call them false beliefs or lies. Whatever you want to call them, the bottom line is that they are *false*. They are not true and they do not serve us. No, this doesn't mean that you are crazy or having a nervous breakdown. In fact, we all have some degree of distorted thinking about ourselves. It's part of our oh-so-helpful (or not helpful, in this case) biology. The good news is that once we develop an awareness that this is what is happening, we can then start paying attention and notice when they come up. There are even different types of cognitive distortions that are broken down into categories. Let's think of them as "thought traps," since it is these negative unhelpful thought patterns that tend to make us feels stuck. Much of what we know about cognitive distortions come from the vast body of research conducted by two widely acclaimed researchers in the field of psychiatry and psychotherapy, Aaron Beck and David Burns. These two psychologists literally wrote the books on depression, cognitive distortions, and the treatment of these problems. Let's take a closer look at the most common negative thought patterns that plague most people at some point in their lives. The first eleven distortions come straight from Burns' *Feeling Good Handbook*:

1. **All-or-Nothing Thinking / Polarized Thinking**

    Also known as "Black-and-White Thinking," this distortion shows up as an inability or unwillingness to see shades of gray (sorry ladies, this is *not* a reference to the soft-core porn novels about Christian Gray). In other words, you see things in terms of extremes - something is either fantastic or awful, you are either perfect or a total failure, and you go all-in or you don't bother doing it at all.

2. **Overgeneralization**

This sneaky distortion takes one instance or example and generalizes it to an overall pattern. For example, a student may receive a C on one test and conclude that she is stupid and a failure and that she should quit school. Overgeneralizing can lead to overly negative thoughts about ourselves and our environment based on only one or two experiences.

3. **Mental Filter**

Similar to overgeneralization, the mental filter distortion focuses on a single negative and excludes all of the positives. An example of this distortion could be, "Because I got one low rating on my evaluation (which also contained several high ratings), it means I'm doing a lousy job." It becomes a "tunnel vision" where we focus only on one part of the situation, ignore the rest, and foster a negative view of everything around us.

4. **Disqualifying the Positive**

On the flip side, the "Disqualifying the Positive" distortion acknowledges positive experiences but rejects them instead of embracing them. For example, a person who receives a positive review at work might reject the idea that they are a competent employee and attribute the positive review to political correctness or to their boss simply not wanting to talk about their employee's performance problems. This is an especially poisonous distortion since it can perpetuate negative thought patterns even in the face of lots of evidence to the contrary.

5. **Jumping to Conclusions - Mind Reading**

   This "Jumping to Conclusions" distortion is a popular one. It shows up as the false belief that we know what another person is thinking. Of course, it is possible to have an idea of what other people may be thinking, but this distortion refers to the negative interpretations that we jump to. Seeing a stranger with an unpleasant expression and deciding that they must be thinking something negative about you is an example of this distortion.

6. **Jumping to Conclusions - Fortune Telling**

   A "sister distortion" to mind reading, fortune telling refers to the tendency to make conclusions and predictions based on little to no evidence and believe them to be gospel truth. One example of fortune-telling is a young, single woman predicting that she will never find love or have a committed and happy relationship, based only on the fact that she has not found it yet. There is simply no way for her to know how her life will turn out, but she sees this prediction as fact rather than one of several possible outcomes.

7. **Magnification (Catastrophizing) or Minimization**

   Also known as the "Binocular Trick" for its clever skewing of your perspective, this distortion involves exaggerating the importance or meaning of things or minimizing the importance or meaning of things. For example, an athlete who is generally a good player but makes a mistake may magnify the importance of that mistake and believe that he is a terrible teammate, while an athlete who wins an MVP award in her sport may minimize the importance of the award and continue believing that she is only a mediocre player.

8. **Emotional Reasoning (i.e., feelings = facts)**

   This may be one of the most surprising distortions to many of you, and it is also one of the most important to identify and address. The logic behind this distortion is not surprising to most people. Rather, it is the realization that virtually all of us have bought into this distortion at one time or another. Emotional reasoning refers to the acceptance of one's emotions as fact. It can be described as, "I feel this way; therefore, it must be true." Of course, we know this isn't a reasonable belief, but it is a common one nonetheless.

9. **"Should" Statements**

Another particularly damaging distortion is the tendency to make "should" statements. This one was my personal favourite, and it is one that I still struggle with and work on all the time. "Should" statements are statements that you make to yourself about what you "should" do, what you "ought" to do, or what you "must" do. They can also be applied to others, imposing a set of expectations that will likely not be met, which ultimately leads to disappointment and frustration. When we hang on too tightly to our "should" statements about ourselves, the result is often guilt that we cannot live up to them (yup… there it is again. Guilt shows up in so many places). When we cling to our "should" statements about others, we are generally disappointed by the failure of the others to meet our expectations, leading to frustration, anger, and resentment.

10. Labelling and Mislabelling

These tendencies are basically extreme forms of overgeneralization where we assign value judgements to ourselves or others based on one instance or experience. For example, a student who labels herself as "a total moron" for failing an assignment is engaging in this distortion, as is the waiter who labels a customer "a crotchety old miser" if he doesn't thank the waiter for bringing his food. Mislabelling refers to the application of highly emotional, loaded language when labelling (translation: lots of cuss words and name-calling).

11. Personalization

Another personal favourite of mine. This one was probably the pattern that trapped me the most when I was in my toxic relationship, and it was extremely hard for me to break out of it. As the name implies, personalization involves taking everything personally or assigning blame to yourself for no logical reason to believe you are to blame (I confess that I was a complete personalization addict for many years). This distortion covers a wide range of situations, from assuming you are the reason a friend did not enjoy a girls' night out, to the more severe examples of believing that you are the cause for every instance of moodiness or irritation in those around you (ding, ding, ding! This was me).

In addition to these basic cognitive distortions, Beck and Burns mentioned a few others as well, and they are known as fallacy distortions.

1. **Control Fallacies**

     A control fallacy manifests as one of two beliefs, (1) that we have no control over our lives and are helpless victims of fate or (2) that we are in complete control of ourselves and our surroundings, giving us responsibility for the feelings of those around us. Both beliefs are damaging, and both are equally inaccurate. No one is in complete control of what happens to them, and no one has absolutely no control over their situation. Even in extreme situations where an individual seemingly has no choices in what they do, where they go, or what they say, they still have a certain amount of control over how they approach their situation mentally.

2. **Fallacy of Fairness**

     While we would all probably prefer to operate in a fair world, this assumption is not based in reality and can foster negative feelings when we are faced with proof of life's unfairness. A person who judges every experience by its perceived fairness has fallen for this fallacy, and will likely feel anger, resentment, and hopelessness when they inevitably encounter a situation that is not fair.

3. **Fallacy of Change**

Another fallacy distortion involves expecting others to change if we pressure or encourage them enough. This distortion is usually accompanied by a belief that our happiness and success relies on other people, leading us to believe that forcing those around us to change is the only way to get what we want. For example, a man who thinks, "If I just encourage my wife to stop doing the things that irritate me, I can be a better husband and a happier person," is exhibiting the fallacy of change.

4. **Fallacy of Always Being Right**

Perfectionists and those struggling with imposter syndrome will recognize this distortion. It is the belief that we must always be right, correct, or accurate. With this distortion, the idea that we could be wrong is absolutely unacceptable, and we will fight to the metaphorical death to prove that we are right. For example, the internet commenters who spend hours arguing with each other over an opinion or political issue far beyond the point where reasonable individuals would conclude that they should "agree to disagree" are engaging in the "Always Being Right" distortion. To them, it is not simply a matter of a difference of opinion. It is an intellectual battle that must be won at all costs.

5. **Heaven's Reward Fallacy**

This distortion is a popular one, particularly with the myriad of examples of this fallacy playing out on big and small screens across the world. The "Heaven's Reward Fallacy" manifests as a belief that a person's struggles, suffering, and hard work will result in a just reward. It is obvious why this type of thinking is a distortion. How many examples can you think of just within the realm of your personal acquaintances where hard work and sacrifice did not pay off? Sometimes, no matter how hard we work or how much we sacrifice, we will not achieve what we hope to achieve. To think otherwise is a potentially damaging pattern of thought that can result in disappointment, frustration, anger, and even depression when the awaited reward does not materialize.

Pick Your Thought Traps

So, now that we have learned about the different types of negative thought patterns that our brains can get stuck in, it's time to identify which of these patterns you are stuck in (and there may be more than one - there are often a few of them that ring true to each person). All you have to do is go back each of these distortions and ask yourself whether it sounds familiar or like something you do. Then, you need to classify how often you think it happens (i.e., rarely, sometimes, often). Write down the distortions that seem to ring bells for you in a journal or in notes on your phone - somewhere where you will see them again. Once we have identified which traps are your go-to patterns of negative thinking, we can start to identify when they are happening so that we can challenge them (more on this later).

It's time to break free from that same old story that you have been stuck in for so long. It's time to create a new narrative, a story that has yet to be told about you and all the brave things that you have done and continue to do, because somewhere inside of you, you ultimately decided that you *are* worth it. Otherwise, you would never have left… so let's go grab a hold of your fears and tackle them together. It's time for you to overcome them and take back control of your mind!

Chapter 7:

OVERCOMING FEAR

In the last chapter, we identified the different fears that are influencing us and the negative thought patterns that we are stuck in. Woohoo! This is half of the battle - truly. Awareness is the key component to change as it is the first necessary step. If we are not aware that we are doing something that is hurting us, it is impossible to change it. Our lack of awareness is often a major factor as to why we feel stuck in a holding pattern of negative thought cycles. So, now that we have an awareness of our fears that feed our false beliefs, what are we going to do about it?

It's simple, really. We are going to use our new-found awareness to help us to notice, challenge, and dismiss our fear-based false beliefs that are holding us back from finding our independence and our confidence in our decision to move on with our lives. To be clear, simple does not mean easy. This will take work and practice, and sometimes that ego voice is going to get really agitated and uncomfortable, and it's going to try to convince us that we need to abort this whole "new life" mission. Don't worry, this is normal, and it is part of the process of growth and change. The important thing is to recognize that this voice is fear-based and therefore *not* based on facts. For those of you who love acronyms, you might find this as a helpful reminder when your fears start to get loud.

F - False
E - Evidence
A - Appearing
R - Real

Key focus on the *false*. I also found the following mantra helpful in times when I have been in total freak-out mode after I ended my relationship. "Just because I *feel* this way doesn't mean it's *true*." I have repeated this to myself over and over on many different occasions, and it helps to ground me and get back in touch with what is *real* versus what I am spinning in my head.

Paying Attention

Okay. Let's take a slow, deep breath, and now we'll begin. The first thing we must do is start noticing when we fall into those negative and distorted thought patterns that we identified previously and recognize the distorted thought. It's important that you give yourself some room for self-compassion here, because you won't pick up on them all right away. It gets easier with practice over time, so, in the beginning, cut yourself some slack (especially all you fellow perfectionists out there)! So, first, we recognize and isolate the thought. How are you supposed to do this? Listen for absolute words, like "always," "never," or "can't." They are usually clues you've got a cognitive distortion going on. So are really strong, negative words that are directed at yourself, such as "hate," "stupid," or "horrible person." Next, you need to write them down. Yes, you really need to do this, and no, you can't record yourself a voice memo. Writing it down on paper really makes a difference, I promise you, and it is a crucial part of getting better at recognizing your distorted thoughts and your fears. Remember, I told you that this would take work, so consider this to be your first written assignment. *Write down the distorted thoughts that you notice.* I don't care where you decide to write it - you don't need anything fancy or elaborate, but you do need to write it somewhere where you won't lose it. Once you've written it down somewhere, you need to take your distress temperature. This is a scale from zero to ten. Zero means you are feeling calm and peaceful, and ten means that your misery is paralyzing.

Tracking Your Thoughts

Once you have rated yourself on the scale, ask yourself, "Is this thought reasonable or unreasonable?" If you are not sure how to evaluate this, I found the easiest way is to say the thought out loud and then consider whether you would agree or disagree with it if a friend were to say that to you. For example, if you have the thought, "I'm such a horrible person for leaving," say this out loud to yourself and think about a close friend or family member saying this to you. Would you believe that they were horrible for leaving a toxic relationship? My guess is that you would say no. If the answer to this question is "no," then it is an *unreasonable* thought. Once you've identified that it is an unreasonable thought, you need to identify what feelings you have that are associated with that thought. Do you feel angry? Sad? Defeated? Hurt? Hopeless? Helpless? Overwhelmed? Write it down beside the thought. Next, decide what kind of cognitive distortion it is. All-or-nothing thinking? Fortune-telling? Take a look at the list and figure it out, because chances are you have a pattern going on. Once you have the distortion labelled, you will be in-tune more easily to when it happens again in a different context. Next, on the same piece of paper, write down a more reasonable thought to replace the distorted one. If you can't come up with anything, think about what you would say to your friend or family member if they said this to you, or think about what the "angel" would say to the cognitive distorting "devil." *Do not* dismiss the response that you come up with a "yeah, but…." This is another thought trap loop that dismisses the positive and only focusing on the negative.

Some people find it helpful to set up their paper in a chart format, to make it easier to keep track of the distorted thoughts as they notice them. Here is an example:

Thoughts	Feelings	Cognitive Distortions?	Alternative, Rational Response
(Write down the repetitive thought)	(List any emotions that you feel when thinking those thoughts)	(Is there a cognitive distortion(s) in your thought? If so, write it down; there may be a few.)	(Think of a more rational response to your cognitive distortion and write that here.)
Example: "I'm a horrible person for leaving."	Anxious, sad, self-loathing	Labelling	"Actually, I'm not a horrible person. I did what I had to do for my well-being and safety."

Chart adapted from *The Feeling Good Handbook* (1989)

Now, retake your distress temperature. Even if it's just a few degrees lower, say, from a nine to a seven, you are going in the right direction, and that's a good thing. Repeat this process as needed. Do not expect to be completely free from your cognitive distortions right away. *That* would be unreasonable (I'm hilarious, I know). However, the more you do this exercise, the easier it will become, and the better you'll get at replacing those negative thoughts with reasonable ones.

Challenging Your False Beliefs

Another way to dismiss our false beliefs is to challenge them. To do this, we must question our perception of reality. This can sometimes feel scary and unsettling, especially when we start to realize and see our faulty thinking patterns. Here are examples of questions I have asked myself to really figure out if my negative thoughts are factual or false:

1. How do I *know* that this thought is 100% true?

2. What evidence/proof do I have to support this belief?

3. Am I comparing this situation to previous ones?

4. Am I assuming that I can't do anything to change my situation?

5. Am I overgeneralizing?

6. Am I predicting the future?

7. Am I focusing only on the negative side of the situation?

8. How is this thought or belief helpful to me?

9. Am I assuming the worst case possible?

10. Am I blaming myself for something that is not actually my fault?

11. Am I taking this situation personally?

12. Are these standards that I hold myself to reasonable? Would I have these same expectations of others?

13. Is this situation truly within my control?

14. Am I confusing thoughts with facts?

15. What effect does thinking this way have on me?

16. What are other ways I can view this situation?

This list of questions helped me so much in changing my way of thinking. I will not lie, at first, I became upset when I realized the damage I was doing to myself by not only thinking these negative thoughts but *believing* them. It was also a big shock for me to realize that, although I experienced years of unfair abuse and manipulation, it was actually up to me to react differently. I finally started to see that I can't control others, but I sure can control my own actions and my reactions to my circumstances. In fact, this realization that I had some control over what happened to me was so *incredibly* empowering. I wasn't helpless. I was only stuck in the situation if I *chose* to be… This was my "a-ha" light bulb moment.

Engaging in Therapy

Although these questions are really helpful in learning how to challenge our distorted thinking, it is important to keep in mind that this list of questions *does not* replace therapy, coaching, or other professional help. It is okay to ask for help - in fact, I strongly encourage you to seek out professional help as you work your way through this process, as I did. Being a professional clinical psychotherapist myself, I cannot stress enough how important it is to find someone that you can talk to who is truly unbiased, who does not have an emotional investment in your life (like family members or friends do), and who is trained to help you move your way through these discoveries. Asking yourself these questions can be overwhelming at times, and having trained professional to work with can be of immense help. There will be moments when your questioning gives rise to more questions. That's perfectly normal, and it is part of the process. If you become confused or overwhelmed by it, I invite you to take a step back and allow other professionals to help you.

Becoming a Scientist

By now, you are hopefully aware that these cognitive distortions are based on fear and not on facts, and they only serve to perpetuate feelings of anxiety (which is fear itself). When we are feeling anxious, we tend to believe that things will turn out badly… but what if our "predictions" are wrong? What if the worst *doesn't* happen? Or, even if it did, would it really be the end of the world? This is where I like to challenge my clients to engage in what we call behavioural experiments, because they let us test out whether the negative predictions or beliefs are accurate or true (spoiler alert: ninety-nine percent of the time, they're not). There are many different kinds of behavioural experiments (which can all be found in more detail on the *Psychology Tools* website), but they all have the same purpose. They all allow us to test the validity of our beliefs about ourselves, other people, or the world around us. Maybe they were old beliefs that you had for a long time, deeply entrenched from the patterns of your toxic relationship, or they may be new beliefs that you don't feel sure about. *Hypothesis testing experiments* are a really great way to test our beliefs. Sometimes, we have a very clear idea about what we think will happen if we behave a particular way in certain situations. One way of testing a belief like this is to conduct an experiment. We do this the same way in therapy that scientists do in a lab, by

1. Making a prediction about what we think will happen (forming a hypothesis)

2. Carrying out an experiment that will test that hypothesis (more than once if needed)

3. Examining the results, and going back to Step 1 (making another prediction)

A few ways of testing a hypothesis are to do a survey or to conduct an experiment. You may be thinking, "But how can I do a behavioural experiment?" Quick answer - just like the scientists! We can approach our beliefs just like a scientist approaching a new phenomenon. They are curious and methodical. Here is a step-by-step approach adapted from Psychology Tools that you can try out.

Step 1: Identify the belief to be tested. What is the belief that you have identified that you want to test? Write it down in a single sentence. For example, "If I make eye contact with people, I'll be attacked."

Step 2: Rate the strength of the belief. How strongly do you believe this statement? Rate it from zero percent (not at all) to 100 percent (completely, with all my heart). Sometimes, it can be helpful to give separate ratings for how much you believe it with your head (logically) and how much you believe it with your heart (emotionally).

Step 3: Plan an experiment that could test the belief. Common methods of gathering information to test beliefs are

- Surveys - asking "do other people believe the same thing that I believe?"
- Hypothesis-testing experiments

Step 4: Identify any obstacles that could make it difficult to carry out the experiment. Is there anything that could get in the way of doing the experiment?

- If you need people to be around to help you, who could you ask?
- If it can only be done in a certain place, when can you go there?
- Are there any safety issues? How could you minimize them?

Step 5: Carry out the experiment. This is the part that will require courage. You may want to have someone with you who can encourage you and remind you why you're doing this.

Step 6: Record the results. Every good scientist records what happened.

Step 7: Reflect on your results and re-rate how strongly you believe in the original belief. Once you have done the experiment, go back to your original belief. Read it to yourself and then re-rate how strongly you believe in it now (on a scale from zero to 100).

Love vs. Fear

If conducting behaviour experiments seems like it's too much for you right now, that's okay. You can save that for another time when you feel like it could be helpful and you have the brainpower to engage in that work. There is a more general way that you can evaluate the helpfulness of your thoughts, and it is simple. Figure out your "love vs. fear" chart. What I mean is, sit down with a pen and paper and write down all of the things that you believe that make you feel afraid (e.g., I am not strong enough to do this), and then make another list of the things you believe that fill you with love (e.g., puppies are cute). Then, do the same things with lists of things that you do (i.e., your actions). If you need more guidance with this, Melissa Ambrosini wrote a great book called *Mastering Your Mean Girl*. In it, she walks you through specific exercises that help to identify the things that we think and do that are driven by fear, and the things that we think and do that are driven by love. The goal here is to take steps to reduce the lists that come from fear and increase the lists that come from love. Her style of writing may be a bit "light and fluffy" for some, but the exercises in it, especially in the first section of the book, are very helpful in sorting this out. While I am recommending resources, I also want to encourage you to log in to your Netflix account and watch the fantastic talk by Brené Brown, *Call to Courage*. It's inspiring, honest, comforting, and exactly what the doctor ordered in those dark moments when you feel like giving up. These resources may also help you understand the emotions that are attached to our fears, which will come in handy as we learn to ride the ups and downs.

Chapter 8:

DRIVING THE EMOTIONAL ROLLER COASTER

Now that we have talked about some different ways to start challenging our fears and negative thought patterns, I want to take some time to focus on managing our emotions. I have no doubt that you currently wake up every day to a roller coaster of feelings that go up and down throughout the day, and that you sometimes don't see coming. It may even feel like you're "going crazy," because you may not be used to feeling this kind of emotional Russian roulette. I remember feeling so drained from the feelings that I contended with, especially in the early days after I left my partner. Sometimes, I felt empowered, strong, and relieved that the emotional mind games and manipulation were over; other times, I felt guilty and panicked that I made a horrible decision and that I had to "fix" it. I had periods of intense anger too - anger at him, anger at myself, and anger for the situation. Waves of intense sadness would suddenly crash over me in the most inconvenient places (crying at your desk or in the grocery store aisle, anyone?), and, at times, the anxiety was crippling. My partner was vindictive and had narcissistic traits, and he could not handle that I was the one to leave him, so I was very anxious about what he might do and how he would get back at me. So, yeah, I can totally relate to the wild ride of emotions that you are probably experiencing.

My Favourite Skills

The good news is, since then, I learned incredibly useful skills to help manage my emotions, and I also took training in a specific type of evidence-based therapy that is aimed at helping people with this exact problem, among others. It's called dialectical behaviour therapy (DBT) and it is *amazing*. According to the Centre for Addictions and Mental Health (CAMH), DBT provides people with new skills and strategies "to make their lives feel like they are worth living." I actually strongly believe that learning DBT skills should be mandatory in schools, as they are useful skills for everyone, not just those who are struggling with their mental health. I am not going to give you a crash course in DBT in this book, but in this chapter, I will share some highlights of specific skills that I found incredibly helpful for me when I was in that confusing and overwhelming period of transition of my life, when I was figuring out how to take back control of my life and start over. The goal of learning and implementing these skills is to give you back control over your feelings so they don't take over the decisions that you make.

States of Mind

One of the main assumptions of DBT is that we operate in one of three different states of mind: the Reasonable Mind, the Emotional Mind, or the Wise Mind.

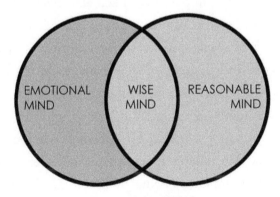

Figure 1: States of Mind.
Modified from the DBT® Skills Training Handouts and Worksheets, 2ⁿᵈ ed. (2014).

The Reasonable Mind is defined as being "cool," rational, and task focused. When we are in Reasonable

Mind, we are ruled by facts, reason, logic, and pragmatics. If you have ever watched *The Big Bang Theory*, Sheldon Cooper's character is represented as someone who is very stuck in Reasonable Mind all the time - he struggles to understand empathy and has a hard time with emotions in general. He places a high value on empirical data and scientific proof rather than on feelings.

The Emotional Mind is the opposite. It is described as "hot," mood-dependent, and emotion-focused. When we are in Emotional Mind, we are extremely reactive and ruled by our moods, feelings, and urges to do or say things. Emotional Mind is impulsive, and facts, reason, and logic are not important. I liken an "angsty" teenager as someone who is often in Emotional Mind, as that is typically the stage of life where a person is learning to sort out and understand their feelings. If any of you are moms to a teenager, first off, you deserve a standing ovation. Parenting teens today is *not* easy, and you deserve accolades for surviving each day. Secondly, you moms will know what I'm talking about when I say that teenagers are prime examples of living in Emotional Mind. "No one understands me or gets how I feel, my parents are stupid, everyone is judging me, I'm *going* to get a tattoo because that will fix everything, woe is me, and music is my life!" In all seriousness, though, being in Emotional Mind means acting on impulses that are driven by how we feel - sending that email or hostile text that you later wish you didn't, smashing something in a rage, and engaging in self-harm activities (e.g., "cutting") because you think it will make you feel better. These are all varying degrees of impulsive behaviours that we tend to engage in when in Emotional Mind.

Wise Mind Rocks

The Wise Mind is where we want to set up camp, because it is the balance of both the Reasonable and the Emotional Mind. The Wise Mind allows us to recognize and respect our feelings while rationally responding to them. The Wise Mind sees the value in both reason and emotion and brings the left and right brain together to synthesize the wisdom within each person. In DBT, the Wise Mind is also known as "the middle path," and the skills that it teaches allow us to get back to our Wise Mind when we are stuck in one of the other states of mind. In this case, it is most likely that you are spending most of your time in Emotional Mind because you are going through a huge life change where emotions are running high. To learn how to take control of your feelings so that they don't get in the way of your decision-making, we will briefly focus on three of the four categories of DBT skills: Mindfulness, Distress Tolerance, and Emotion Regulation.

Learning Mindfulness

Being able to recognize the states of mind and work towards getting back to your Wise Mind is a core Mindfulness skill. However, recognizing which state of mind you are in requires taking a step back, taking a deep breath, and asking yourself, "Am I operating from my Wise Mind right now, or am I in Emotional Mind?" It is important to start *observing* what you are doing or thinking, and then *describe* it to yourself (e.g., "I am pouring myself a fourth glass of wine because I feel sorry for myself and want to wallow in my sadness"). Then, you have enough understanding of what is happening to be able to ask yourself, "Is this really helping me, or is it harming me? What would a person in Wise Mind do?" Practicing these Mindfulness skills allow us to slow down our actions and resist the urges of our impulses. A great Mindfulness mantra to practice saying to yourself is, "Just because I *feel* this way doesn't mean it's true." Light bulb moment: feelings are not facts. When feelings are heightened, they are often not based on reality but on an exaggerated fictional narrative that we created in our minds. To be clear here, I am in no way saying that your feelings are not valid. What I am saying is that our feelings sometimes cloud our ability to see things clearly, and we need to be mindful of how they are impacting our ability to make sound decisions. This is important because how we feel often dictates what we think, and what we think influences what we do. Therefore, we need to check in with how we feel and take steps to keep our feelings in check so that we can see things more clearly and avoid doing things that we will later regret.

When you are practicing these Mindfulness skills, you must do so from a place of *non-judgement*. You will not catch yourself getting swept up in Emotional Mind all the time. You will sometimes not be able to stop your unhelpful actions before they happen. You *will* make mistakes and your emotions will still get the better of you sometimes. That is okay. It is vitally important that you do not beat yourself up when you falter or give in to your impulses. Give yourself permission right now to make mistakes, because it is inevitable that you will. Feeling guilty about making them doesn't help anybody - it just makes you feel like crap. So, let the guilt and the judgement go, and just *notice* when the mistakes happen, analyze what led to them happening, and think about how you can approach a similar situation differently the next time. Be kind and patient with yourself, just as you would with a friend.

Tolerating Distress

Distress Tolerance skills are also vital tools in getting control of our emotions. Distress Tolerance skills are used to help us cope and survive during a crisis, and help us tolerate short-term or long-term physical or emotional pain. The goal of these skills is not to make a situation better but to keep it from getting worse (and to keep you from spiralling down an emotional rabbit hole). They are divided into four different categories of "crisis survival" strategies: Distracting, Self-Soothing, Improving the Moment, and Pros/Cons. We will look at the first three of these categories.

In DBT skills training, Distracting skills are represented by the acronym "ACCEPTS" to highlight the different ways you can distract yourself when your emotions start to feel really uncomfortable:

- A - Activities: exercise, hobbies, cleaning, events, play games, watch movies

- C - Contributing: volunteer work, make a gift for someone, help someone

- C - Comparisons: people less fortunate, others coping less well than you

- E - (Opposite) Emotions: scary/funny movies, joke books, fun music

- P - Pushing Away: leave the situation mentally for a while (put in a box)

- T - Thoughts: count to 10, count colours in a room, puzzles, read, cook

- S - Sensations: hold an ice cube in hands, squeeze a rubber ball, hot shower

Every type of Distracting skill will not work for every person. Some people find one type of skills more effective or powerful than another, which is totally normal. The key is to find a couple of groups of skills that work best for *you* and help you to stay grounded in the uncomfortable feelings. Self-soothing skills incorporate your five senses to help you calm down when feelings are heightened and intense. Engage your visual senses by watching something on TV, reading a book, looking at art, or observing things in nature. Engage your hearing by listening to sounds outside, music, radio, or a podcast. Engage your sense of smell by cooking or baking something with an aroma, diffusing some essential oils, lighting a scented candle, going for a walk, or smelling the freshness of nature. Engage your sense of taste by chewing gum, eating dark chocolate, or drinking cold water. Engage your sense of touch by wearing soft clothing, petting an animal, exercising, getting a massage, or practicing yoga.

Improving the Moment skills can help us manage difficult emotions during stressful situations and regulate our emotions in the present moment. The important thing to remember (another mantra, perhaps?) is that these intense emotions don't last forever. You can use these IMPROVE skills (the DBT acronym for them) to tolerate emotions until the intensity subsides:

- **I - Imagery**: e.g., imagine relaxing scenes, a safe place, pain leaving your body

- **M- Meaning**: e.g., focus on the positive that this current pain brings

- **P - Prayer**: e.g., ask your Wise Mind / a higher being for strength to bear the pain

- **R - Relaxation**: e.g., tense and release your muscles, take a bath, get a massage

- **O - One** thing at a time: e.g., focus only on the sensations of washing the dishes

- **V - Vacation**: e.g., turn off your phone, go away for the day, go to the beach

- **E - Encouragement**: e.g., be your own cheerleader ("I can do this! I've got this!")

The distress tolerance techniques found in IMPROVE can be used anywhere and anytime you need to tolerate a situation that you can't change. Practicing these techniques during minor situations will help them to come to you naturally when bigger problems arise.

Regulating Your Emotional Thermometer

Lastly, I'm going to briefly share some Emotion Regulation skills that literally saved my sanity when I was in the depths of emotional turmoil after ending my relationship. The goals of Emotion Regulation training are to gain a better understanding of the feelings we experience, reduce our vulnerability to being overtaken by our emotions, and decrease emotional suffering. The main emotions that tend to become "out of balance" are love, anger, fear, joy, sadness, and shame. Emotion Regulation skills help us to bring our emotional state back to balanced (i.e., back to our Wise Mind) or keep it from getting out of balance. When you notice that you're experiencing an emotion, observe it without judgement. While some emotions may be more pleasant than others, each is valuable. Identify the emotion you're feeling and consider what this emotion may be trying to tell you about your situation. Then, you can decide whether to listen to the emotion or let it go.

The first set of Emotion Regulation skills in DBT is called ABC PLEASE (in the past, these skills were known as "PLEASE MASTER"). These skills are used to decrease our vulnerability to experiencing unwanted emotions.

- **A - Accumulating positive experiences.** By regularly participating in activities that we enjoy and setting and working toward long-term goals, most of the negative experiences we have won't seem as detrimental.

- **B - Build mastery.** This skill reminds us to constantly work on improving ourselves and our talents. As we learn and master a new hobby or skill, we feel successful and accomplished regularly. We become more confident and learn that we can be successful in other areas as well.

- **C - Cope Ahead.** We are often aware of the situations that will make us uncomfortable before they happen. Coping ahead helps us to prepare in advance for these situations. If, for example, you have a test coming up, you can prepare ahead by studying, talking with your teacher, and identifying a self-soothing skill to use during the test. This preparation will likely decrease the anxiety you feel before and throughout the exam.

- **P + L** - Treating **P**hysica**L** illness

- **E** - Balanced **E**ating

- **A** - **A**void mood-altering recreational drugs

- **S** - Balanced **S**leep

- **E** - **E**xercise for 20 minutes a day

The ABC PLEASE skills are guidelines to help us take care of our physical health since our physical health is closely tied to our mental health. When we are sick, exhausted, or otherwise unhealthy, we are more susceptible to negative emotions. By caring for our bodies, we increase the likelihood of a more positive emotional experience.

The Emotion Regulation skill of "Opposite Action" helps us take control of our emotions when they don't fit the facts. Each emotion we experience comes with an action urge, or behavior, associated with it. After identifying the emotion you're experiencing, try to identify the associated behavior. For example, if you are feeling ashamed, the behavior that follows might be isolating yourself from others. If you are feeling happy, the behavior might be smiling. Often, these action urges feel like they make sense for the situation you're in. These urges often intend to protect you, but our emotions aren't always right. For example, feeling afraid before public speaking and having the urge to run away doesn't fit the situation. Public speaking does not put your life in danger (there are no tigers!); therefore, you don't need to run away. When the emotion doesn't fit the fact or the situation, we need to identify an action that *opposes* our emotional urge rather than an action goes along with it. Using our shame example, if you're feeling ashamed and feel the urge to isolate yourself, the opposite action could be to intentionally seek out the company of a safe friend and share your shame. While this may be easier said than done, you will definitely feel better afterwards, and doing this will be much less destructive to your life and current situation.

FYI, Opposite Action is most effective when it's done "all the way," meaning that you act opposite in thoughts, words, and deeds. Although it's hard at first (believe me, I get it), it's important to continue practicing opposite action until you start to feel differently. Eventually, the action urge will be replaced with a new, more productive action. Because you now know how to counter the urges of your uncomfortable emotions, they'll be easier to tolerate and you will bounce back to your Wise Mind more quickly. Each time we practice an emotion regulation skill, we decrease the likelihood that a negative emotion will severely impact us. These skills help us understand that we actually *do* have some control over the emotions that we feel and how they impact us.

Understanding and managing our emotions can seem like a scary and daunting concept - believe me, I've been there, too. What I love about these skills is that they are logical and concrete, which is the opposite to how our emotions feel sometimes. They also are easy to start using - all it takes is practice and a conscious effort and awareness. Using tangible skills like these also makes our emotions feel less out of control or overwhelming (which is my goal for you) to feel less overwhelmed by your emotions. Learning how to take back control of your feelings will also allow you to function better in all areas of your life. This will also help improve your self-confidence, especially as you start to branch out and meet new people.

Chapter 9:

MAKING CONNECTIONS

One of the hardest things about ending a relationship, regardless of how unhealthy it was, is the loss of that person who you knew was always there. Even if you didn't really want them to be there, in the end, there was some kind of twisted comfort that there was *someone* close to you, who knew all of the things about you. To suddenly go from seeing this person every day of your life to only seeing them or talking to them when necessary is a really big shock to the system similar to someone dying. One day they are there, and the next day they are not. Truthfully, ending a relationship is very similar to a death in many ways, and it is normal to grieve the loss of someone so close to you even though they were not good for you. There is a sudden gaping hole in your network, in the inner-most circle of connections that we have created. For me, it felt paralyzing. I am a social person and my friendships are important to me, so losing the person to whom I was once closer than anyone else in this world was *brutal*. I don't think it really matters whether you're introverted or extroverted, or if you have lots of friends or few friends - losing your partner is just plain *hard*.

To recover from this loss (and all of the toxic feelings that went along with it), I knew that I would have to find new connections with different people. At first, I probably did it just to fill that deep dark void that I felt inside. But after some time passed, I began to start feeling whole again. That void was getting filled in with all kinds of goodness : compassion, caring, and love from people who were not a part of my life before. I believe whole-heartedly that the connections that I made in my first four months living in the Dominican Republic were what saved me from falling into a deep and lasting depression from knowing that my relationship was over. Yes, I chose to end it, but that doesn't mean it is easy or that the feelings of loss are not there. By the time it was all said and done, my cup was empty. I needed to make new connections and create a new support network for myself that was uniquely *mine* and that would help me to fill my cup back up again. My Dominican family and friends turned out to be exactly who I needed to come into my life at that time, and I thank God that I was put into their path to find, welcome, embrace, and love me.

Finding New People

Is moving to another country the only way to find a new support network? Of course not! It just so happens that I had the unique opportunity to go there for humanitarian and teaching work, so I took it. There are *many* other ways to build a new community and support system around you. Some of you may be fortunate to have family members who live close by and who you are close to, and this is definitely the first line of support for a lot of people. However, if you're like me, you may live far away from your family, or you may feel like your family has its own interpersonal issues that get projected onto you. This isn't helpful or supportive to you in your situation at all (this was the case for a few clients who were going through the process of ending and leaving their abusive relationships). Even if you do have family member support that you actually want, I always recommend finding other connections within an outside network or circle. I know that your brain is likely going into excuses mode ("But I can't make outside connections, because…"), and I am going to call it out right now. There are actually *zero* legitimate reasons why you cannot find ways to connect with new people and cultivate meaningful relationships. To prove this to you, I am going to highlight just *a few* of the options that exist for making new connections with like-minded people. Are you ready?

Volunteering

The first thing that I did was get involved with a volunteer service organization in my community. These organizations exist in every city and in most towns all over the world. Rotary clubs, Kiwanis clubs, Lions clubs, and Optimists clubs have been around for several decades and do well-known work all over the world (e.g., End Polio Now is a project of Rotary International, partnered with the Bill and Melinda Gates Foundation). New-generation service clubs, such as the HandsOn Network and dosomething. org, are popping up all over as well. What do these clubs do? Well, they are voluntary non-profit organizations where members meet regularly (weekly, bi-weekly, or monthly) to plan and carry out charitable projects, either by direct, hands-on efforts or by raising money for other organizations. Becoming involved in Rotary was what opened the door for me to be able to start doing humanitarian work in the Dominican Republic. I applied for a volunteer service grant and was approved, which covered my living expenses for the first four months that I was there. Rotary also provided me with opportunities to improve my public speaking abilities and become involved in creating and running several high school volunteer clubs. I even organized international volunteer service trips for students to take part in. Long story short, getting involved in a service club literally changed the course of my life for the exponentially better.

If joining a service club isn't your thing or doesn't fit into your schedule at this time in your life, but the idea of volunteering interests you, there are so many ways that you can get involved and give back to your community. Boys and Girls Clubs, Big Brother/Big Sister, and food banks/soup kitchens are always looking for new volunteers. Seniors' centers or retirement homes also love to have outside people come in to do activities with the senior residents. Animal shelters need people to come and spend time with the animals there, and animal rescue organizations are always looking for foster families to house the animals until they get adopted to a forever home. If you are looking for a way to give back, I *promise* you there is an opportunity for you to do so. All you have to do is ask Google to help you find the right thing for you. The bottom line is that volunteering or joining clubs brings you into a group of like-minded people instantaneously, so it is a great way to meet new people quickly.

Taking a Class

Maybe volunteering is not possible for you right now, or maybe it's not an interest that you have currently with everything else that is going on in your life, and that's fair. Maybe taking a class is more what you are looking for. Again, the options here are pretty much endless: fitness classes (spinning, body pump, kickboxing, Orange Theory Fitness - if you've never gone to a workout at an OTF you *have* to check it out), yoga practices, art classes, music classes, sewing/knitting classes, cooking classes, craft classes, cake decorating classes - there are *so many* choices! The key is to find something that speaks to you and sparks your interest, and to sign up and *go* to the class. This is another easy way to be put in a room with other people who have a common interest with you. Whatever you're into or whatever you want to learn how to do, just get out there and join in on a class. Once you are there, you can start talking to people. Over time, you'll get to know them and create some great new connections. Joining a community support group, such as Al-Anon, Nar Anon, mood disorders peer support, or grief and loss support (among many others that exist) may also be really beneficial, especially if you are have survived or lived through addiction, loss, mental health issues, or other significant life challenges. Each group is set up differently, some with group counselling as part of the programming and others with more sharing, peer support, and encouragement. Peer support groups are another easy way to be in a room with a group of people who have gone through something similar to your experience, which you may find comforting and helpful.

There's an App for That

Not feeling the whole going-to-a-class thing? No problem - the internet has you covered.

Another tool that I found incredibly helpful when I was trying to "find my people" after moving home from the DR was the MeetUp app/website. You may already know about it, or maybe you've heard of it but haven't actually checked it out, or maybe this is the first time someone has told you about it. Regardless, it is an excellent tool for connecting people and bringing people together who enjoy similar activities. Not so fast, my shy and introverted friends - they even have MeetUp groups for introverts (as I said, there really is no excuse)! It is really simple and easy to use; all you have to do is create an account with your email, and search where you live. They have groups divided into categories of interest (e.g., outdoor adventure, photography, food and drink, crafts, book clubs, fitness), and within each category there are multiple groups that you can join. These are more focused on specific kinds of activities or specific groups (e.g., girls' night out for fifty-plus, chess club for ages twenty to thirty-five). You can choose to get emails when there is a new event created in one of the groups that you belong to so that you can RSVP if you are interested. I used this app in three different areas of the country, and a client of mine even uses it when she goes on vacation so she can join in on a cool excursion wherever she is visiting (I love this idea, by the way, and I am totally going to start doing this).

Speaking of apps, another client of mine, who struggled with social anxiety and low self-confidence, taught me something cool about the Bumble app. I totally thought that this was strictly an app for dating, like Tinder or Match, but Bumble has taken it to the next level by also offering the same service to meet new friends and for business networking as well. So cool, right? Back to my client. She is a stay-at-home mom of two young kids (which, I believe, is one of the hardest jobs in the world), and she had a really hard time finding ways to get out on her own and meet people in classes, etc. because she has her kids all the time. So, she decided that she wanted to connect with other moms who were also feeling a bit isolated, and she was able to make some new mom friends through using the BumbleBFF feature on Bumble! This enabled her to start chatting with other mothers. She got to know them, and then they started getting together *with* their kids - everybody won!

Online Communities

Facebook groups can also be great ways to find virtual or online support if getting out of the house is tricky for you, or if the idea of joining in a gathering (even with other introverts) is too daunting right now. Online support groups or online interest groups are a great way to virtually connect with people who are going through a similar experience, or who are also looking to connect but aren't able to physically get out to activities. For example, I know that Facebook has several support groups for women who are going through separation and divorce (try searching for things like "Divorced women support" and "Uplifting Support for Divorced, Single Women"). Other organizations offer virtual communities and message boards depending on your interests. Being a part of an online community can be helpful for sharing resources, getting non-judgemental peer support, and sharing ideas of how to cope and take the next steps on your journey.

A New Social Network

No matter how you prefer to meet people, the key is that you put yourself out there even if you feel tired, or annoyed, or whatever other excuse comes up for you when you think about creating a new circle of friends. We are a social species and it has been proven over and over that we do not do well when we are isolated. Even the most introverted of people require a sense of social belonging to feel fulfilled and happy. *So*, this means that it is actually pretty crucial that you force yourself to reach out and connect to *some* kind of community… and you never know where those connections will take you. Remember, we are working on building "You 2.0," so we don't want to be doing the same old thing with the same old people all the time. It's time to branch out and see what social network awaits the "new" you!

Chapter 10:

"WHO AM I, ANYWAY?"

Up to this point, we talked a lot about specific actions and strategies to help us to get a hold of our emotions, identify and work through our fears and false beliefs, and make sure we are taking care of ourselves in various ways. These are all crucial and necessary steps that we need to take in our journey towards healing, independence, and having a new life all on our own. However, one of the biggest realizations that I get from clients in our sessions (and the biggest realization I had myself as well) is, "I don't even know who I am anymore." Yup... heavy, isn't it? There is this moment of clarity that comes when sorting out all of the piles of emotional baggage and turmoil, when you have a quiet moment to yourself. That is when you realize that, in all of the years of chaos, hardship, and heartache in the relationship, you've lost touch with or forgotten who *you* are as a person all to yourself (not a mom, or a partner, or a volunteer, or an employee). Think back to a time before you entered into this relationship, and back to a time in your life when you didn't have to really be responsible for or to anyone else. What were you like back then? Think about the things you used to do, the things that brought you *joy* (à la Marie Kondo), and the things that you were passionate about. What were the things that used to define you? For me, I remember feeling like I was so broken and so far from who I used to be, and I had no idea how to find *that girl* again. It was so long since I felt true passion and joy for anything, or the desire to express my creativity through music or poetry, as I used to do every day. I felt like a hollow shell of a woman - as you probably do - whose essence was sucked out of her. So, how can we get *that girl* back and then some? How do we launch a re-boot of "Me: 2.0?" This is what we're going to talk about now.

Making Your Power Playlist

First thing's first, we need a power playlist. Not just any playlist with some of your favourite tunes. We need a "pump-me-up-so-much-I-feel-like-Wonder-Woman-*and*-Beyoncé" playlist. Even better, we need to start this playlist off with a theme song - your theme song. If you're a Madonna fan (like me), I've got you covered. My theme song was "Jump." This was my opening song on my power playlist. Then, I added other songs that also feel empowering to me. More and more get added to it over the years as new songs come out that really speak to my inner power. Aretha Franklin's "Respect," Beyoncé's "Rule the World (Girls)," Gloria Gaynor's "I Will Survive," Lady Gaga's "Born This Way," Rachel Platten's "Fight Song," Pink's "Raise Your Glass," and Katy Perry's "Roar" are just some of the tunes that come to my mind from my current go-to playlist that helps to remind me that I *can* do hard things, I *am* worthy, and I *am* worth it.

Revisiting the Past

Okay. Now that we have our soundtrack playing, let's get back to work. Who were you before you entered into this toxic relationship? What were you really good at doing? What were those things that you used to love, that brought you joy? I want you to get out some paper and a pen and jot your answers to these questions down in bullet-point form - put the book down and go do it right now! Don't overthink it - just jot down anything and everything that comes to mind. Once you have your answers/lists made, look at what you've written. What do you wish you still had in your life? Which things do you really miss and want to reconnect with? For example, music was a big one for me - playing the piano and the guitar, going to live music events, singing, and song writing. Maybe you loved drawing, painting, making crafts, engaging in a sport, or writing. Maybe animals used to be a big part of your life, or maybe travelling or reading for pleasure. Start by picking one thing that you want to have back in your life and consider the ways that you can make it happen. It might not look the same as it did before (e.g., if you owned a horse before but cannot have one now, find a stable or a farm nearby that you can visit), but that's okay. What matters is that you are reconnecting with a part of yourself that got lost. Once you get back into a groove with it, then you can look at another thing on your list that you want to revive. Slowly and surely, those lost parts of you will start to come alive again.

Learning - and Doing - Something New

If your old interests are truly not calling to you anymore, this is a great opportunity for you to engage in some new activities or hobbies, like learning how to run, training for a triathlon, learning how to knit, joining a book club (the MeetUp app can help you find one), or deciding to learn a new skill (e.g., learning a foreign language or how to play a musical instrument). One of my clients decided that she was going to start learning how to do small home renovation projects despite her husband always telling her that her ideas wouldn't work, that she would just make a mess, or that she couldn't do it properly. She had all of these really great ideas for changes that she wanted to make around the house, but she never felt like she could because she knew her husband would mock her or put her down in some way. One day, in a session when we were talking about this, she just looked at me and said, "Screw it! I'm picking up the drill, and I'm doing it!" This was *such* an empowering moment for her, and I wanted to leap out of my chair, give her a high five, and yell, "Freaking right!" (This may have happened.) Since then, she has built cubby stations in her mudroom to house the explosion of her kids' things when they come through the door, painted and re-decorated a bathroom (and hung floating shelves, mirrors, and cabinets), and re-painted the main foyer of her house. She watched YouTube videos for the things that she was not sure how to do and she just went for it. Her renovation work is beautiful, and she is so proud and surprised to learn that she *can* do these things that she has always wanted to do no matter what anyone said to her in the past.

Whatever it is that you decide to try, it is so important to stick with it for at least a couple of months to see if you like it. I decided to learn how to run and train for my first half-marathon and to learn Spanish. My motive for learning Spanish was not only out of interest, but I also decided that I was going to go spend some time volunteering in a Latin country for a few months (and then ended up going back to live there for almost two years). I know that moving to another country for a period of time may not be possible for everyone and that it can be harder to navigate with children. However, I can honestly say that doing this was what helped me to really reconnect with myself - living far away from everyone and everything that I knew, in a foreign-speaking country with customs and value systems that were so different than my own. I was completely out of my element in *every* way, and I had no one else to rely on but myself. I suddenly found myself with a lot of alone time on my hands, and, at first, I didn't know what to do with it. I was uncomfortable with this time at first, but, slowly, I began to really process through the years of emotional abuse and aggression that I survived, the very messy and dramatic end, the false beliefs that I had developed about myself - all of it. I had space away from the noise of my previous life (though there was *plenty* of noise pollution in this country - it was just different noise, in Spanish!), and this allowed my nervous system to start to calm down. This made it possible for me to process through some of those really painful memories and recurring thoughts using the skills that I learned in therapy before I left Canada.

Moving On

I appreciate that moving to a foreign country may not be realistic for some people, but I encourage you to think about how you can truly get some distance and "unplug" yourself from your everyday life - even if it is only for a few days here and there - as your life and schedule will allow. Alternately, think about whether it is possible for you to move, even if it is not that far away, so that you can have that feeling of a fresh start, a clean slate, with no toxic memories there to immediately haunt you. If you can't move, consider how you can create a sense of newness and unfamiliarity in your life: take a different route to work, change up how things are arranged in the house, paint some walls, get a new car, or re-arrange your kitchen. Challenge yourself to live in a "new" environment, however that looks. It is in that experience of newness where you will start to feel the real parts of you coming back to life.

Giving Back

Another great question for us to reflect on is, "Where and how can I have an impact on the world?" For me, this was an easy answer. I had a strong calling to become involved in international development work, and I was able to answer that calling through Rotary International. My initial four months there eventually led to a five-year project in one of the remote sugar cane villages where I used to teach. From there, I became connected with locals who started a grass-roots non-profit organization to provide foreign groups with a cultural immersion and development project experience. After years of proposals to the school district where I taught in Canada, finally I got approved to bring high school student groups to the Dominican Republic to participate in this life-changing program. Six years later, there are now four schools from that school district who continue to participate in these programs.

So, what is your calling? Where do you want to make a difference in the world? Maybe it's through coaching a local sports team, mentoring a trainee at work, or helping with a breakfast program at a local school. Maybe you already found it and engaged in it for years (way to go!). If you're not sure what your calling is, go back to that list of answers that you made and reflect on what you are *passionate* about. Then, think about ways that you might be able to engage that passion in some way that gives back to others. Giving back to others can be a very powerful gift, as it cultivates healing and the ability to let go of our own pain.

Sending Yourself Some Love Mail

Finally, one of my favourite exercises that I love to give to my clients who, like you, are searching to find out who they are and what makes them happy, is to ask them to write a letter to their future self one year from now. Write to yourself as though you are writing to your closest friend. In your letter, include your hopes for her one year from now: what she'll be doing, positive life changes she will make, new people she'll met, cool things from the bucket list that you hope happened. Include words of encouragement for her and share where things are with you now, today, so that she will be able to see how far she came from this place. Remind her of the things that you love, admire, and respect most about her. Remember, you are writing as though to your closest friend, so this last part shouldn't be too hard - think about what you'd say to that closest friend. You can also respond to questions that you ask your future self. For example, what does your life look like daily? Where do you live and what is the quality of your life? How do you feel about yourself? What are you most proud of? What are the experiences that you had that added the most value to your life? This future letter-writing is an exercise backed by research, too. A study from New York University professor Hal Hersfield found that, when people can realistically imagine their future selves in a clear and positive light, they are increasingly able to make choices that will benefit that future self. I love this exercise as a way to discover who we really are, because it helps to get our thoughts out of the present and keeps us focused on what is yet to come. Manifestation, baby! So, I invite you to sit down, take in a deep breath, and start writing. Your future self is waiting.

P.S. |If you are feeling particularly pumped by this section, here are a few more resources for you to check out that I highly recommend:

Girl, Stop Apologizing - Rachel Hollis
Made for More documentary - Rachel Hollis
(via Amazon.com)
Take Control of Your Life - Mel Robbins (Audible only)

Chapter 11:

FINDING YOUR VOICE

I am so excited that you have started to find your true self again, and reconnect with the *real* you. Welcome back, sister! Now that you have regained a sense of yourself, who you are, and who you are working towards becoming, it's time to talk about your voice. I'm talking about that part of you that wanted to speak up, fight back, or just scream *so many times* when you were being abused, manipulated, or hurt by your partner - the part that wanted to stand up for yourself but was too afraid of what might happen. It may be many years since you last felt that you even had a voice; it's time to give that part of you the centre stage and the microphone.

Mindset Matters

To do this, we first need to look at what kind of mindset you are working from: a victim or a warrior. A victim mindset operates from a place of powerlessness and helplessness, frozen in the place where past traumas or abuse happened and blames everything and everyone else around them for their circumstances. A victim makes excuses for things that they do or don't do and typically complains about everything. A warrior is someone who is still fighting, clawing their way back to a "normal" life. Being a warrior means turning our pain into a purpose. A warrior eventually becomes a survivor; someone who is back to that sense of normalcy in her life, and she carries the mindset that, if she was able to get through what she just did, then nothing can break her.

I have found myself in both categories, at different times in my life, but what I've come to realize is that we have the power to *choose* to switch from the victim to the warrior, at any given moment - and this is an incredibly empowering and calming truth. Now, I am not suggesting that it is possible to always fully live from the warrior mentality; after all, breaking down and crying is cleansing and healing in itself. Life may not always be easy, but the choice we do have at each second is to be willing to see things differently. So - I invite you to consider which mentality you are adopting today: the victim or the warrior? This choice will make *all* the difference in how you show up to the world.

Warrior Women

Let's take a look at a couple of well-known examples of women who decided to show up as warriors. The first person who comes to mind every time I think of a #warriorwoman is Tina Turner. You may be familiar with her story, but in case you're not, here is the "Reader's Digest" version (you can also check out her 1992 biopic movie, *What's Love Got To Do With It?*, or her latest memoir, *My Love Story*): basically, Tina's rise to fame took place under the thumb and almost constant threat of her abusive ex-husband, Ike Turner. The physical and sexual abuse that she sustained regularly has been well-documented, and he nearly killed her on more than one occasion, by brutally beating her repeatedly and forcing intercourse on her. After years of enduring this, she stood up for herself and left Ike in 1976, and has such a powerful message of hope and life after abuse for all women around the world. Next up is my ultimate girl-crush: Lady Gaga. She revealed in an emotional awards acceptance speech (and also in an interview with Howard Stern) that she was sexually assaulted at the age of nineteen, and her songs *Swine* and *Til it Happens to You* are based on her experience and living with the aftermath. Since sharing her story with the world, she has become a vocal advocate for the #metoo movement and all survivors of abuse. What makes these women, and so many others like them, warriors rather than victims, is that they decided to use their experience to make change in the world, to create something positive out of something horrific, and to look forward, rather than stay stuck in the past and be poisoned by the bitterness and unfairness of what happened to them.

Chances are, if you're reading this book, you're a warrior too, as you've already demonstrated your strength by having the courage to walk away from your abusive and toxic relationship. If you're anything like me, though, it probably doesn't *feel* like you're a warrior, and you probably have moments where you question your worth - I know I did. To be able to find our voice, it's important that recognize that we *are* worthy; worthy of happiness, joy, independence, peace, love - all of the things! So, how do we start to feel and believe this to be true? First, we need to figure out our 'positive qualities' (yes, you totally have them). Get out your notebook, and jot down the first answers that you can think of for the following questions, adapted from researcher Courtney Ackerman:

- What do you like about yourself, however small or 'insignificant'?

- What have you achieved in your life, no matter how small?

- What challenges have you faced - and overcome?

- What gifts or talents do you have (no matter how small)?

- What skills have you acquired (e.g., knitting, cooking, changing a car tire)?

- What do other people like or value in you?

- What qualities and actions that you value in others do you have?

- What aspects of yourself would you appreciate if they were aspects of another person?

- How would someone close to you describe you?

Once you've got these answered, I want you to list all of those positive qualities on another sheet of paper; beside each one, write down a past example of when you demonstrated each quality. You don't have to do these positive things absolutely perfectly or 100 percent of the time (that is impossible), so it's really important to be realistic about what you write down. Once you have listed some past example, start keeping a daily journal of your positive qualities daily. Each day, try to record three examples from your day that demonstrate certain positive qualities that you have. Write exactly what you did and identify what positive attribute it shows in you. Writing down the specific incidents that show your positive qualities will start to have a positive impact on your view of yourself, making it feel more real and believable.

Affirming Your Worth

I also love the power of creating self-love statements and positive affirmations. Affirmations for self-esteem are a great way to build our confidence and self-worth, especially when they are repeated over-and-over again. By repeating these positive mantra-like statements each day, you start to believe in the truth behind them; this helps to boost our confidence, and when we start to believe, we begin to make these statements true. If you're not sure how to get started or what to write for your first positive/self-love statements, try practicing a few of my favourites, and then work on creating your own:

- I deserve to be happy and successful.

- I deserve a good life.

- I am competent, smart and capable.

- I am growing and changing for the better.

- I love the person I am becoming.

- I am worthy of all the good things that happen in my life.

- I am confident with my life plan and the way things are going.

- I let go of the negative feelings about myself and accept all that is good.

Repeat your affirmations aloud for five minutes, three times a day - morning, noon and night. This repetition will slowly help to internalize and start to believe them. After practicing this repetition for a couple of weeks, I challenge you to say them to yourself while looking in a mirror. According to Louise Hay, the founder of mirror work, the most powerful affirmations are those we say out loud when we are in front of the mirror. This is because the mirror reflects the feelings we have about ourselves. The reason why this is called mirror *work* is that it is extremely uncomfortable at first. Sitting in front of ourselves in a mirror is hard to do, as we are very self-critical; however, as you continue to practice saying these self-love statements to yourself, it becomes much easier over time and our reflection will start to become a friend rather than an enemy or someone we are afraid of.

What's the Point?

So why does all of this self-love stuff matter? It matters because we need to learn to stand up for ourselves and to believe that we have the right to do so when our boundaries have been crossed. Learning how to say "no" to abusive or disrespectful behaviour is one of the most difficult and simultaneously empowering lessons that I've ever experienced. One way to practice doing this, without any risk of negative consequences from other people, is to write a letter to your ex, highlighting everything that you wish you could have said in the past. When you sit down to write this, make sure you've got uninterrupted time, and that you can also freely let out any emotions that you need to, as you write. Don't hold anything back - this is your opportunity to speak up, to use your voice, and stand up to that person who was so threatening and who wielded that power over you. This is not a letter that you need to send; this is a way for you to finally say all the things that you couldn't. After writing this letter, I invite my clients to read it aloud in a session, if they feel that they want to, so that they can practice *saying* the words to another person, in a safe space. Perhaps you can share it with a close friend or a family member if you are not currently working with a therapist. Once they are done with it, many clients shared that they decided to burn it, as kind of a "cleansing" ceremony, a cathartic release of all of the negative emotions and toxicity that had been kept inside for so long.

Once you've had some practice standing up against inappropriate behaviour, in a safe space, you can start to practice asserting yourself with other people. After writing her letter, one of my clients decided that she was going to start calmly dismissing the disrespectful way her ex-husband spoke to her. She shared with me that a comment I made in a previous session stuck with her - that people will treat us the way that we teach them they can. When we don't speak up to people who talk down to us, threaten us, demean us, or disrespect us, we are reinforcing that we accept this behaviour as being okay and that they can continue to treat us that way. This realization was a big light-bulb moment for this client, and it pushed her to find the courage to start standing up for herself. Each time her ex made a degrading, rude, or hostile comment, she pointed out that she was speaking calmly, and that there was no need for him to react in such a disrespectful way, and that he no longer has the power over her that he once did. She also started to ignore him, at times, and she stopped showing him that his words had any impact on her, emotionally. She continues to do this, and it has allowed her to start to feel confident in herself again. What she said to me, more recently, at the end of a session, is a message that I want to share with you, in the hope that it will resonate with you: "Even though everything feels messed up sometimes, I *know* that I'm okay, and I know now that I'm worthy of respect." Yes, she is - and so are you.

Learning how to use your voice and stand up for yourself is one of the most important tools that you will ever have. Your voice is your power, and you do not have to apologize for using it when you are being mistreated by *anyone*. Using your voice makes the difference between the victim and the warrior. When you say nothing, you are choosing to be a victim, and when you learn how to speak up, you are choosing to be a warrior. I want you to start choosing to be the strong warrior princess that is there inside of you, because once you set her free, there will be nothing she cannot overcome.

Chapter 12:

THE BUMPS AND THE POTHOLES

For the last eight chapters, we walked through the steps of personal growth that are integral in creating a new and independent life living on our own after ending an abusive and toxic relationship. I've shared some real-life examples, ideas, and exercises for how to implement each of the steps to make it as seamless a process as possible. However, I realize that this work cannot take place in a vacuum. Outside forces will always be at play in your life, whether they be other people, work, or unexpected life circumstances. The universe can be ironic sometimes. Right after I declare that I'm going to do something, a huge obstacle will suddenly pop up to make it more difficult. However, this is *not* just cause for giving up on this work. In this chapter, I want to acknowledge and discuss some common obstacles that may come up for you and get in the way of stepping into your power, and why you *need* to find your way to the other side of whatever they are. I also want to highlight the cost of avoiding this work, the value in doing it, and, finally, the opportunities available to you if you decide to use the skills in this book and engage in this personal growth work.

Obstacles

One of the biggest obstacles to implementing these steps is something that we tend to put up ourselves, the classic tried-and-true excuse of "not having enough time." As women, in particular, we seem to have perfected the art of putting everything and everyone else's needs ahead of our own and filling in every minute of the day with tasks that "need" to be completed. I was guilty of this myself, at different times in my life, when I really needed to focus in on myself and what I needed to be okay in that season. I prioritized the needs of my family and friends, work demands, school requirements, volunteering, cleaning the house - pretty much anything and everything, actually, and I deemed these things to be more worthy of my time than my own self-care and personal growth work. In my practice, I often hear mothers, in particular, that they just don't have enough hours in the day to possibly do work for themselves that they need to do. The reality is, we all have the same twenty-four hours in the day, and it is simply a matter of revisiting priorities and effective time management (the latter also being something that I struggled with, and still do at times). Rather than scrolling through the newsfeed on Instagram or Facebook for forty-five minutes, we could be listening to a guided meditation, journaling/reflecting on the fears that came up for us that day and practice challenging them, doing some personal growth reading, watching a TedTalk on the things we are struggling with, or practicing positive affirmations in the mirror - you get the idea. If you were to stop and write out *everything* that you did in one day and how long you spent doing each activity, I guarantee you that would be shocked at how much time you would suddenly be able to find by cutting out things that eat up our time and serve no helpful purpose. Our mental health is vital to being able to hold all the other responsibilities and stresses in our lives together. The choice is up to you as to whether you're going to prioritize your well-being over checking in with what the Kardashians are doing.

A similar trap that we tend to fall into is wrapping ourselves up completely in the needs of our children and using them as an excuse as to why we "can't" work on ourselves. After leaving a toxic relationship, we tell ourselves that we must focus 100 percent on the kids, *their* emotional well-being, and how *they* are handling this transition, and there's simply nothing else that matters. If you don't have kids, replace focusing on their well-being by throwing yourself 100 percent into your work and becoming a workaholic. Perhaps you feel like working all the time and "staying busy" will be good for you so that you don't have to pay attention to those intrusive thoughts, intense feelings, or the reality of the situation. That's a *great* plan until you finally crawl into bed exhausted and, just when you close your eyes, all those things come rushing into your mind all at once. The truth is, no matter how busy we force ourselves to become, avoiding the things that are holding us back from getting to a place of thriving on our own and loving our independence will only bring us more pain and, possibly, long-term negative effects that will be much harder to deal with later.

Another hugely common obstacle that can get in the way of getting to work (if we let it) is continuing to allow other people to define or control you or, in other words, continuing to care about what *other people think*. I get it, fear of judgment is real, and it can feel very overwhelming. But being scared of upsetting others or being judged for having the courage to leave and start a new life on your own is actually letting those other people control you. Maybe you've got over-bearing or very traditional family members, nosy neighbours, or gossipy coworkers, but who they are doesn't matter, and what they think matters even less. You just got out of a toxic relationship where you, quite likely, felt like you were being controlled in some way by your partner. *Why* would you then go ahead and not *do* anything about rebuilding a life that you want because of what other people might say or think? Remember, fears are not based on facts - they are based on the fiction that we write in our heads. We have no idea what other people think about our situation (nor is it any of their business, quite frankly). Even if you do know that someone is upset about the choice you're making, it's not *their* life, it's yours, and you get the chance now, finally, to learn how to live the life that you want.

What's at Stake

If I'm being completely honest with you, there are probably hundreds of obstacles that could prevent us from engaging in the work we need to do after leaving a toxic relationship if we go looking for them. In the end, we are the ones who are in control of whether we ultimately recover from the ordeal we have been through, and learn how to live independently and happily, or whether we stay stuck - stuck in all of the pain, the hurt, the resentment, and the fear that haunts our minds and poisons our hearts. If we let those obstacles that we find get in the way of learning to thrive and be independent on our own, the outlook doesn't look so rosy. Yes, it might feel easier to do nothing at this moment right now, but the end result leads to a final destination of living out that "victim" narrative, blaming everything and everyone else for all the problems and injustices that we encounter in life. This road to Bittertown is a lonely one, as we usually do a pretty good job at alienating everyone who cares about us along the way, and we arrive feeling utterly alone, damaged, and betrayed. For some reason, as I am typing this, images of scenes from Tim Burton's *The Corpse Bride* are coming into my head - scenes where the people from the underworld are the ones who live in colour, laughing, loving, and dancing (even though their physical scars, injuries, and open wounds are fully exposed). Meanwhile, the people on Earth are living in black and white, prisoners to their rigid societal rules, principles, judgments, and perceived slights. They live in bitterness, fear, and constant discontentment with their lives. Although initially these images made me giggle a little, the more I think about it, I believe it is exactly the visual example that I am looking for - making the best of a bad situation and finding ways to thrive in new circumstances (like the dead people in the Underworld), or focusing on the negative so much that it becomes a part of who we are to the point where we are miserable all the time (just like the "real" people above the ground).

Avoiding this work also has negative implications for the other relationships in your life, particularly children, if you have any. Similar to the car that is never brought in for repairs, tune-ups, or basic maintenance and then performs poorly or breaks down, neglecting our own necessary recovery, healing, and growth results in us showing up as hollow, broken down versions of ourselves in all of our roles: as a parent, coworker, friend, and family member.

Everything continues to feel incredibly overwhelming, and the pain morphs into bitterness over time. This will also likely reinforce ideas that we are not good enough, smart enough, or worthy of happiness, and that the world is conspiring against us in some way. We also run the risk of never going after or realizing our dreams and goals that we had set a long time ago, as we become stuck in that perpetual cycle of bitterness and believe that we are destined for failure.

What's It All Worth?

As you made your way through the different chapters in this book, you may have thought (more than once) that this all seems like a *lot* of work, and you're right. Self-reflection, self-care, naming and challenging fears, regulating emotions, and reaching out to others is hard work. This may deter you from wanting to put in the time and effort that is required to learn how to grow as an independent woman on your own, but let's continue on with our cost/benefit analysis.

Remember when I told you about the huge sum of debt that my ex made sure I had to pay, and I chose to look at it as the cost of my freedom? You may be wondering how I was able to do that, and the answer is simple. I asked myself what my freedom was worth to me - being free from the disrespect, gaslighting, manipulation, fear, and feelings of constant guilt for making small "mistakes" or my "misunderstandings." When I thought about that, it became clear to me that I reached the point where I was pretty much willing to do *anything* to escape all of it, and finally feel like I could live my life without walking on eggshells or worrying about what might him upset. Following the steps outlined in this book to reclaim your life as an independent person living on your own are the same steps that I followed, too. I believe, with every fiber of my being, this is a worthwhile investment of your time and energy. The value of what you stand to gain from engaging in this work is priceless. This is *your life*, and you have the opportunity now to re-build it and create it in the way that you want, that honours *your* needs, values, and goals.

Then there is the incredible example and life lesson for your children. You've already shown them that it's okay to leave a relationship if there is no respect. Now it's time to teach them that it's *okay* to do things to take care of yourself and that it's possible to have a great life after the end of a relationship. They are looking to you to follow your example, so why not include them in the journey and share these skills with them as well? This what you have longed for so many times, when you were trapped back in that toxic relationship that was slowly chipping away at the core of your being. Are your freedom, independence, and happiness worth a few months of hard work? *Abso-freaking-lutely*!

New Opportunities

Not only will engaging in these steps to reclaiming your life give you new strength, more clarity in your future, and better mental health, but it also allows for new opportunities to come into your life as you are ready to accept them. A new job, city, or friendships; exploring the world and learning new skills - the possibilities for you are endless. Establishing that belief in yourself again (or maybe for the first time ever) is the key to unlocking a window of endless opportunity. I *know* that you will be amazed at what new and exciting things await your discovery. You have so many strengths, abilities, interests, and tenacity inside of you - if you didn't, you wouldn't be reading this book! I truly hope that you can hear my heart when I tell you that you are *so much more* than you think you can be, and this is why I am cheering you on to break through the barriers and obstacles to completing this work. Your inner "Wonder Woman" is waiting for you to discover her and release her to the world, and I can't wait to see what happens when you do.

Chapter 13:

FROM PAIN TO POWER
AND PURPOSE

When I first met you, way back at the beginning of this book, I found you on a life raft, floating in a vast and infinite sea of confusion, emotion, and fear. You had the courage to leave an intimate relationship that was abusive, toxic, and no longer serving you. You got on your life raft and paddled hard to get away, and then you probably felt exhausted and overwhelmed, and you've been floating on that sea ever since. Since you likely didn't know me yet, I decided to introduce myself and share my story of how I recovered and found a new life on my own after getting out of my own toxic relationship. I also told you about some of my psychotherapy work with other women who were going through the same things. I hope that this brought you some comfort in knowing that you are not alone, that others have gone before you, and that we can relate to your struggles.

After we became acquainted, we began to move through a series of eight steps that were designed specifically for you, as you worked to figure out how to live on your own again and (re)gain your independence. We started by looking at the roadblocks that were getting in the way of moving forward. This is where you met your ego voice, who is in charge of making sure that you feel fear and uncertainty about your decision to leave the relationship. We then moved on to the importance of self-care, what that means, and many examples of ways to start taking care of yourself and being kind to yourself right away, just as you would encourage a friend to do. We looked at how vehicles need regular care and maintenance to perform well and avoid breakdowns and discovered that we are more like a car than perhaps we ever thought. To show up as our best selves for others, we need to put our own care and maintenance work first.

Next, we identified the lies and all the limiting false beliefs that we were carrying around for many years. We learned how perpetuating these beliefs was holding us back and started working on noticing them when they came up. We walked through concrete exercises to help you to notice, challenge, dismiss, and overcome these fears and distorted thought patterns and discussed the power of positive affirmations and belief in ourselves. We also spent time working on regaining control over our emotions, as this whole experience that you've been through has been a roller coaster of mixed emotions that probably have felt, at times, out of control. We learned about mindfulness skills, states of mind, distress tolerance skills, emotion regulation skills, differentiating thoughts from feelings, and allowing room for the grieving process to take place as you mourn the loss of the relationship and a significant other in your life. We also talked about the importance of making new connections and creating a support network that is uniquely your own, and different ideas for how to go about reaching out and meeting new people. We are inherently social beings, and even those of us who are more introverted still need a support system in place. We need understanding, positive, and supportive people in our lives, period.

Finally, I invited you to reflect on the question, "Who am I, anyway?" The answer may not have been clear. In fact, the answer may have been that you had no idea anymore. I invited you to remember and consider things that you used to love doing, way back before you got involved in your toxic relationship, and to think about the things that bring you joy and make you smile. This is where I asked you to write a letter to your future self and include all of the things that you hope are in place for her one year from now. I also highlighted the importance of finding your voice again so that you can stand up for yourself and teach people how you want to be treated, so that you never accept abusive or disrespectful behaviour again. I asked you to consider the mindset that you are in, whether it be the "victim" or the "warrior" and the differences between the two. We looked at some examples of women who survived horribly abusive intimate relationships and used their painful experiences to create awareness, advocacy, support, and inspiration for all women. I also invited you to start practicing positive affirmations so that you can find your inner warrior and become your own version of Wonder Woman for this next phase of your life.

My goal in writing this book was to provide you with a road map to recovery, healing, and learning to live independently with confidence after leaving a toxic relationship. I created this because I know that I would have greatly benefitted from a step-by-step guide that showed me the way to rebuilding my life at a time in my life when I needed it most, when I was barely able to hold it all together and go about my daily requirements. Most importantly, though, my purpose for this book is to leave you feeling hopeful and inspired to take these action steps towards your own personal growth journey. My hope is that this will help you to find your way from your life raft to solid ground and to know that, although this is one of the most difficult times in your life, it also incredibly exciting and empowering.

As you take your next steps towards your new life, my wish for you is that you can start to believe in yourself, to find your inner confidence and believe in your worth, your talents, and your gifts that you have to offer the world. I want you to be able to create a life that is, perhaps for the first time ever, truly *yours* - a life that you want and that you do not have to apologize for or justify to anyone. My wish for you is to find your stride in your new-found independence and create a life that brings you all the hope, happiness, and success that you deserve - where the bright days far outnumber the dark days. In this process, I hope that you find ways to let go of any guilt or shame that was lingering and that it is replaced with self-compassion and love.

"I now see how owning our story and loving ourselves through that process is the bravest thing that we will ever do." Brené Brown is right - learning to love yourself and believe that you are worthy of goodness and love in your life is the ultimate measure of bravery and courage. Just as Tina Turner, Lady Gaga, and so many other warrior women who came before us did, it's now *your* time to step into your courage, roll up your sleeves, and turn your pain into your power and, ultimately, your new purpose. You are *so much stronger* than you think, and the life that you have always dreamed of is now before you, waiting for you to jump in. Are you ready? Take my hand, and let's *go!*

Acknowledgments

First, I must thank the women who inspired me to write this book. To my dear friend Tricia, who found her voice and decided to live her very daring truth, you inspire me every day. To my many amazing clients, who have been so courageous in realizing and following their truths, I feel so blessed to be a part of your incredible journey. To Cassidy, who demonstrates wisdom and strength well beyond her years, and who remains a shining example of resilience and bravery. I am humbled and amazed by each of these women every day.

To my parents, who supported me in this completing this whirlwind journey, and who encouraged me and cheered me on in all of my endeavours. Thank you so much for all that you do for me.

To my sister, who has always been a powerhouse woman in my eyes. She has always gone after her professional goals with grit and tenacity, and persevered and triumphed over so many obstacles that were put in her way. Thank you for being such a wonderful example of never giving up and fighting against hypocrisy and patriarchy, and for being such an inspiration for me to look up to.

To Josh, who supported me each day as I moved through this process, and always did whatever he could to make my life easier even when I didn't want him to disrupt his life. Whether it was cooking, cleaning, creating a beautiful space for me to write, or spending many hours entertaining himself while I worked, thank you for always helping me willingly and selflessly.

To Linda and Matt, who took on the added responsibility of looking after my four-legged companion whenever I needed to travel without him to make the publication of this book happen. Thank you so much for always taking such wonderful care of my beloved Jaguar.

To Bob and Margaret, who have given me a tranquil home away from home to come to whenever I need. Your beautiful home and hearts were the haven I relied on the most while in the process of writing this book. I am so blessed to have you both in my life.

To Debbie and Erin, who are Author Incubator alumni. If it were not for the two of you, this book would surely not have happened. Debbie, thank you so much for sharing your experience and encouraging me to follow my gut and embark on this journey of The Author's Way, and for your continued friendship and support afterwards. Erin, thank you for reaching out, collaborating with me, and sharing your wisdom and knowledge with me as I was progressing through this program, and for encouraging me along the way.

To Dr. Angela Lauria and her amazing team at the Author's Academy. Thank you so much for believing in me, in my book, and in my message, and for providing me with the opportunity to participate in this incredible life-changing experience. To Ramses, Cheyenne, Ora, and Moriah, thank you for all your guidance, support, and wisdom in helping me to create this book. You are all so patient and gifted in the work that you do, and I will be forever grateful for it all.

Finally, Thank you to David Hancock and the Morgan James Publishing team for helping me bring this book to print.

Thank You

Iam so grateful that you decided to spend some of your precious time with me as you read *I Left My Toxic Relationship - Now What?* I love your bravery and your commitment to building a new and happier life for yourself. Since you've finished reading this book, I know that you are on your journey to independence and living on your own again after everything you've been through.

As a thank-you for reading, I have created a free class for you to take today to catalyze your next steps in rebuilding your life. Visit http://toxicrelationshipbook. com to access your class.

I am so passionate about linking arms with other women and helping them to find their power as they take their next courageous steps towards starting their new lives. I would love to learn more about your journey and success in rebuilding your life. Please keep in touch with me on social media (I'm most active Facebook and Instagram), share your wins (tag me and use #frompaintopower), and visit http://toxicrelationshipbook.com for more resources, programs, and upcoming events.

Call to Action!

To take a Self-Care Questionnaire, please visit
www.toxicrelationshipbook.com

About the Author

Heather Kent is a registered psychotherapist and certified teacher from Nova Scotia, Canada, with a background in trauma assessment and treatment. Working with clients locally, nationally, and internationally, much of her professional private practice is focused on helping women through the process of ending abusive and toxic relationships and rebuilding their lives after they have left. Having survived her own experience in a toxic relationship, Heather soon came to realize that many other women find themselves in the same situation, which leaves them feeling broken, ashamed, and alone. During her time living in the Dominican Republic, she discovered another phenomenon of emotional manipulation and abuse that is commonplace among the tourist areas of the country, where foreign women on vacation are taken advantage of and conned by charming and charismatic local men who work in the tourism industry. Seeing women become trapped in these situations further reinforced her desire to help women to escape these toxic relationships and learn how to thrive on their own.

Heather completed her master of counselling psychology degree at the University of Calgary and went on to complete various trauma training programs and certifications. She also holds a bachelor of education degree from Queen's University and was a practicing grade school and post-secondary educator for over a decade. Heather combines her experience from her previous teaching career with her integrative therapeutic approach to counselling. She develops individualized treatment plans in collaboration with her clients to help them to overcome the various challenges that they are faced within their personal and professional lives. Through her online programs, speaking engagements, workshops, and retreats, Heather serves a larger population of clients who are looking for interactive, guided support from a licensed professional as they navigate their way through the end of a bad relationship and the beginning of the next phase in their lives.

Though currently residing in Ontario, Heather is a true Cape Bretoner at heart and returns to her home island on the east coast of Canada every summer. She comes from a long line of strong, independent women, following in the footsteps of her grandmother, mother, and older sister, who have dedicated their careers to helping others. Heather has been an advocate for social justice since her high school days, whether it be for animal rights, human rights, or international development work. She joined Rotary International through a local Rotary club in 2008 and has been actively involved in humanitarian projects, both locally and abroad, ever since.

In her spare time, Heather likes to keep active. She loves running, swimming, hiking, paddling, and skiing with her partner, and loves spending as much time as possible outside in nature, especially in summer. She also enjoys helping people with other aspects of health and wellness, with a particular focus on nutrition. Above all, Heather is a dog-lover and devotes much of her time and energy to her beloved Labrador retriever, Jaguar.

9 781642 799873